Max Herz, Stanley Lane-Poole

Catalogue of the National Museum of Arab Art

Max Herz, Stanley Lane-Poole

Catalogue of the National Museum of Arab Art

ISBN/EAN: 9783744794862

Printed in Europe, USA, Canada, Australia, Japan

Cover: Foto ©Thomas Meinert / pixelio.de

More available books at **www.hansebooks.com**

CAIRO

Sketches of its History, Monuments, and Social Life.
By STANLEY LANE-POOLE,
Author of 'The Art of the Saracens in Egypt,' 'Studies in a Mosque,' &c.

With Numerous Illustrations on Wood by G. L. SEYMOUR and others; and a Plan of Cairo, showing the positions of the Principal Mosques.

The Times.—'As good wine needs no bush, so Mr. Lane-Poole needs no merit but his own to recommend his work on Cairo.... Very charming illustrations.'

The Saturday Review.—'Will prove most useful to the innumerable travellers who now every winter visit the Nile valley.'

The World.—'A most interesting as well as valuable publication.'

Daily Telegraph.—'Most interesting and instructive sketches of the history, monuments and social life of this ancient city.'

Manchester Guardian.—'This beautiful book ... of so many fascinating chapters is a thing to accept gratefully.'

The Scotsman.—'A volume full of entertaining and instructive pictures—written with abundant learning, but in an easy, popular and readable style.'

Liverpool Mercury.—'Likely to become the favourite authority for Cairo.'

The Guardian.—'Its pages are crowded with elegant and careful illustrations of architecture, scenery and characteristic types of mankind. Mr. Lane-Poole has poured out freely into these pages the wealth of his knowledge of things new and old.'

LONDON: J. S. VIRTUE & CO., LIMITED,
26, Ivy Lane, Paternoster Row, E.C.

CATALOGUE

OF THE

NATIONAL MUSEUM

OF

ARAB ART

BY

MAX HERZ BEY

CHIEF ARCHITECT OF THE COMMISSION OF ARAB MONUMENTS
CURATOR OF THE MUSEUM

EDITED BY

STANLEY LANE-POOLE, M.A.

HON. MEMBER OF THE COMMISSION OF ARAB MONUMENTS

Author of 'The Art of the Saracens in Egypt,' 'Cairo,' 'Studies in a Mosque,'
'The Mohammadan Dynasties,' 'The Speeches of Mohammad,'
'The Moors in Spain,' &c.

WITH ILLUSTRATIONS

LONDON
BERNARD QUARITCH, 15 PICCADILLY

TO HIS HIGHNESS

ABBAS II
KHEDIVE OF EGYPT

THIS WORK IS, BY PERMISSION,

RESPECTFULLY DEDICATED

BY THE AUTHOR

CONTENTS

	Room	Page
PREFACE	.	ix
AUTHOR'S NOTE .		xiv
CHRONOLOGICAL TABLE .		xv
INTRODUCTION		xix
STUCCO, STONE, AND MARBLE	I & Annexes	1, 91
METAL-WORK . . .	II . .	18
,, . .	VII .	77
,, . .	Passage	86
,, . .	Annex I	89
GLASS . . .	III . .	30
TEXTS, etc.	,, . .	44
WOOD-CARVING AND INLAY, etc.	IV	45
,, ,, ,,	V .	60
,, ,, *meshrebīyas*	VII	75
,, ,, ,, etc.	Passage .	83
	& Annex I .	89
POTTERY .	VI . .	64
BOOKBINDINGS . .	VIII .	79

ILLUSTRATIONS

	PAGE
Slab from a Prayer-niche. I, 19 .	face 10
Marble jar and stand. I, 34, 108 . . .	11
Inlaid silver and brass kursy. II, 12 . .	face 23
Inlaid silver and brass kursy of En-Nāsir. II, 13 ,,	24
Koran case, brass inlaid with silver and gold. II, 57	face 25
Enamelled glass lamp of Sultan Hasan. III, 20 .	35
Enamelled glass lamp, xivth c. III, 38 . .	38
Enamelled glass lamp of Sheykhū. III, 76 .	42
Bronze lantern, 1419. III, 130 . .	face 44
Kursy of inlaid ivory and ebony. IV, 59 .	face 55
Carved side of a Sheykh's tomb	55
Mihrāb of Seyyida Rukeyya. IV, 62 . .	face 56
Panelled door of Ashrafiya. IV, 64 . . .	56
Filigree bronze lantern, xivth c. IV, 66 .	57
The Kaaba in enamelled tile-work. VI, 167	71
Enamelled tile. VI, 172	72
Panel of Meshrebīya. VII, 1	76
Door from el-Azhar. Passage, 1 . .	face 83
Brass lantern. Passage, 86 . .	87

NOTE.—A few of the above are reproduced from Lekegian's plates in the French edition of the Catalogue.

PREFACE

The traveller who visits the temples of the Nile has not seen all the art of ancient Egypt: he must supplement his view of the monuments by a study of the matchless collections of the Gīza Museum. In the same way, it is not enough to make the round of the mosques of Cairo: one must also visit the Arab Museum. As the Gīza collections illustrate the ancient art by their classified series of objects found in the tombs or rescued from the sand, so the Arab Museum contains those remains of the Saracenic art of the past twelve centuries which have been gathered from the ruins of vanished mosques and palaces. The introduction of a bastard European style, the laying out of new streets, and the broadening of old ones, during the past fifty years, are responsible for more havoc among the monuments of Saracenic art than the centuries of former neglect. The street fights of Mamlūk Beys and Turkish Pashas did less damage to the mosques of Cairo than the futile attempt to Europeanize a medieval Eastern city. The ruins of demolished buildings became the happy hunting-ground of collectors and dealers, and the Museums of Europe and the houses of dilettanti are full of the spoils.

At last the Government of Egypt, which had already placed restrictions upon the exportation of the relics of ancient art, began to take notice of the spoliation of the Mohammadan monuments, and concert measures for the preservation of the remains of the national art. There was a project for an Arab Museum in 1869, when the Khedive Isma'il authorized Franz Pasha, then chief architect of the Ministry of Wakfs, to select a suitable building; but the plan fell through, and it was not till 1880 that the East arcades (or *līwān*) of the Mosque of El-Hākim were appropriated to the reception of objects of Saracenic art. The task of organizing the new Museum was again placed in the able hands of Franz Pasha, who in 1883 removed it to its present place in the court of the same mosque.

With the appointment, at the close of 1881, of the the "Commission for the Preservation of the Monuments of Arab Art," the Museum entered upon a new and more active phase. Among the leading members of this Commission were scholars, archaeologists, and architects, such as His Excellency Yakub Artin Pasha, the present Under Secretary for Public Instruction, Franz Pasha, the late Rogers Bey, and MM. Bourgoin, Baudry, and Grand Bey; besides the English officials of the department of Public Works, first Sir Colin Scott Moncrieff, and now Mr. W. E. Garstin. The Commission, to which alone we owe the present greatly improved supervision and preservation of the mosques and other buildings of Cairo and elsewhere in Egypt, was empowered by the late Khedive not only to watch over the monuments and execute such repairs as were necessary to their preservation, but also to transport to the Arab Museum any fragments or detached objects of artistic or historical value which could not be protected in their original position. The ruins of mosques and palaces, which were beyond the resources of restoration, were carefully searched for such remains, and these form the chief materials of the collections now exhibited in the Museum.

The objects differ essentially from those in most public collections, inasmuch as they are nearly all relative,—dependent upon the monument to which they once belonged,—and were seldom designed as separate works of art. All Saracenic art is decorative, or subsidiary to architecture; and the collections of the Arab Museum consist mainly of portions of the decoration and furniture of mosques and private houses,—such as carved and inlaid doors, sculptured stone and plaster ornament, painted ceiling-joists, bronze filigree plating, marble mosaic, and other substantive parts of the architectural decoration, every piece of which was designed in relation to the main structure. Even detached objects, like the splendid series of enamelled glass lamps, which is the special glory of the Museum, and the exquisite filigree bronze tables inlaid with silver, however beautiful in themselves, were strictly connected with some mosque and in harmony with its decorative style. But this relativity of the Arab Museum collections in no wise detracts from their beauty or interest. On the contrary, it is only from such specimens of ornament as are there preserved that we are able to study some of the more obscure periods of Saracenic art. The Museum contains fragments which reveal the style and ornament of several vanished mosques of periods hardly represented by any standing monuments. And whilst the carved and inlaid panelling of a door, or the rich colouring of a ceiling, inevitably reminds one of the irreparable loss of the building it once adorned, each individual panel or painted joist is itself a marvel of artistic design and skilled handicraft, and suggests valuable motives and developments to the student of ornament.

To study connectedly the history of Saracenic ornament as elaborated in Egypt, the Museum requires to be arranged in strict chronological order. This is manifestly impossible in the present crowded building, already overflowing into two annexes. Plans for a new Museum, with which the Khedivial Library will be combined, have been approved, however, and by 1898 we may hope to see these unique collections worthily housed.

Meanwhile the present catalogue provides ample evidence of the historical and technical knowledge which Herz Bey, who has been curator of the Museum under the Commission since 1892, is qualified to bring to the arrangement and explanation of the collections in his charge. His constant and zealous energy in the work of preserving the Arab monuments, as chief architect to the Commission, has earned him the gratitude of every lover of Cairene art; and the present catalogue increases the debt. The original edition appeared in French in 1895; but it was felt that the large and yearly increasing number of English and American visitors to the Museum called for an English version. The catalogue in its present form has been somewhat condensed: Herz Bey's valuable introductions to the various sections have been in some degree recast; the orthography of Arabic names has been made uniform with that adopted in my *Art of the Saracens,* and the Egyptian sound of hard g is used for the letter *jīm*; but in other respects the catalogue itself is substantially unchanged. I hope it will induce every English and American visitor to study the exquisite national art of medieval Egypt, of which the Arab Museum, after the mosques, offers the most complete representation now attainable in Cairo. The study may be continued with advantage among the rich Saracenic collections of the British and South Kensington Museums, which present many objects of rare interest and beauty.

STANLEY LANE-POOLE

The Athenaeum,
  Pall Mall,
    1 *Jan.,* 1896

AUTHOR'S NOTE

On the 20th April, 1892, the Commission for the Preservation of the Monuments entrusted me with the charge of the Museum of Arab Art. For five years previously, since the retirement of H. E. Franz Pasha from the administration of the Wakfs in 1887, the Museum had been without a special curator, and the collections had been allowed to fall into some disorder. My first care was to revise the inventory and re-number the objects. I then drew up a brief MS. catalogue, which was placed in the galleries for the use of the public. But as the number of visitors increased year by year, I considered it desirable to prepare a fresh *catalogue raisonné*, which should not merely enumerate, but supply an historical and technical commentary on the various objects. For their provenance I have relied upon the original inventory of Franz Pasha. In the detail of the descriptions, I have made it a special point to accurately record the Arabic inscriptions; and here I must acknowledge the valuable assistance of Yusuf Efendy Ahmad, the draughtsman to the Commission, who possesses a wide knowledge of Arabic calligraphy, and has often been able to reconstruct mutilated inscriptions. I should like also to mention the services rendered by Aly Efendy Bahgad, of the Ministry of Public Instruction. To Yakub Pasha Artin, who has taken a true scholar's interest in the Museum from the beginning, I am indebted for such information as his Excellency is peculiarly fitted to give.

HERZ

CHRONOLOGICAL TABLE

A.D.	RULERS	MONUMENTS
639—641	Conquest of Egypt by 'Amr	Mosque of 'Amr, 642, frequently restored
641—868	Governors (98) appointed by Caliphs	

TŪLŪNIDS

868	Ahmad ibn-Tūlūn	Mosque of Ibn-Tūlūn, 876—8
883	Khumāraweyh	
895	Geysh; 896 Hārūn; 904 Sheybān	
905—934	Governors (13) appointed by Caliphs	

IKHSHĪDIDS

934	Mohammad El-Ikhshīd	
946	Abū-l-Kāsim; 960 'Aly; 966 Kāfūr; 968 Ahmad	

FĀTIMID CALIPHS

969	El-Mu'izz	Foundation of El-Kāhira (Cairo), 969
		Mosque El-Azhar, 971
975	El-'Azīz	Azhar made a University
		Mosque of El-Hākim, 990—1012
996	El-Hākim	
1020	Ez-Zāhir	
1035	El-Mustansir	Gates and 2nd wall of Cairo, 1087
1094	El-Musta'ly	

CHRONOLOGICAL TABLE

A.D.	RULERS	MONUMENTS
1101	El-Āmir	Mosque El-Akmar, 1125
1130	El-Hāfiz; 1149 Ez-Zāfir	
1154	El-Fāïz	
1160	El-'Ādid	Mosque of Talāi' ibn Ruzzīk, 1160

AYYŪBIDS

1172	Salāh-ed-dīn (Saladin)	Citadel and 3rd wall of Cairo
1193	El-'Azīz; 1198 El-Mansūr	
1199	El-'Ādil (Saphadin)	Tomb of Imām Esh-Shāfi'y, 1211
1218	El-Kāmil	Medresa of El-Kāmil, 1224
1238	El-'Ādil II	
1240	Es-Sālih Ayyūb	Medresa and mosque or Es-Sālih, 1242
1249	Tūrān Shāh	Tomb of Es-Sālih, 1249

MAMLŪKS (BAHRY OR TURKISH)

1250	Queen Shejer-ed-durr	
1250	El-Mu'izz Aybek	
1257	El-Mansūr 'Aly	
1259	El-Muzaffar Kutuz	
1260	Ez-Zāhir Beybars	Mosque of Ez-Zāhir, 1268
1277	Es-Sa'īd Baraka Khān	
1279	El-'Ādil Selāmish	
1279	El-Mansūr Kalāūn	Māristān and mosque of Kalāūn, 1284
1290	El-Ashraf Khalīl	Portal of En-Nāsir brought from Acre
1293	En-Nāsir Mohammad. (1st reign.)	
1294	El-'Ādil Kitbughā	
1296	El-Mansūr Lāgīn	Restoration of mosque of Ibn-Tūlūn, 1296
1299	En-Nāsir Mohammad. (2nd reign.)	Medresa of En-Nāsir, 1299

CHRONOLOGICAL TABLE

A.D.	RULERS	MONUMENTS
		Restorations of El-Azhar, El-Hākim, tomb of Es-Sālih, Tulūi', etc. 1302
		Khānkāh of Beybars, 1306
1309	Beybars el-Gāshenkīr	
1310	En-Nāsir Mohammad. (3rd reign.)	Mosque of En-Nāsir in Citadel, 1318
		Medresa of Sengar El-Gāwaly and Salār,1323
		Mosque of Kūsūn, 1329
		Mosque of El-Māridāny, 1338
1341	El-Mansūr Abū-Bekr	
1341	El-Ashraf Kūgūk	
1342	En-Nāsir Ahmad	
1342	Es-Sālih Ismā'īl	
1345	El-Kāmil Sha'bān	
1346	El-Muzaffar Hāggy	
1347	En-Nāsir Hasan. (1st reign.)	Mosque of Aksunkur, 1347, restored by Ibrāhīm Āgā, 1652
1351	Es-Sālih Sālih	
1354	En-Nāsir Hasan. (2nd reign.)	Mosque of Sheykhū. 1355
		Mosque of Suyurghātmish, 1356
		Mosque of Sultān Hasan, 1358
		Restoration of El-Hākim, 1359, and El-Azhar, 1360
1361	El-Mansūr Mohammad	
1363	El-Ashraf Sha'bān	Medresa of El-Gāy El-Yūsufy, 1372
		Mosque of Umm-Sha'bān, 1368
1377	El-Mansūr 'Aly	
1381	Es-Sālih Hāggy	

b

MAMLŪKS (BURGY OR CIRCASSIAN)

A.D.	RULERS	MONUMENTS
1381	Ez-Zāhir Barkūk	Medresa of Barkūk, 1384
1399	En-Nāsir Farag (interrupted by 'Abd-el-'Azīz, 1405)	Tomb-mosque of Barkūk, 1405—10
1412	El-'Ādil El-Musta'īn ('Abbāsid Caliph)	
1412	El-Muayyad Sheykh	Mosque of El-Muayyad, 1420
1421	El-Muzaffar; Ez-Zāhir Tatār	
1421	Es-Sālih Mohammad	
1422	El-Ashraf Bars-Bey	Medresa of El-Ashraf Bars-Bey, 1423
		Tomb-mosque of El-Ashraf Bars-Bey
1438	El-'Azīz; Ez-Zāhir Gakmak	Mosque of Gakmak, 1453
1453	El-Mansūr 'Othmān	
1453	El-Ashraf Īnāl	Tomb-mosque of Īnāl, 1456
1461	El-Muayyad Ahmad	
1461	Ez-Zāhir Khōshkadam	
1467	Ez-Zāhir Temirbughā	
1468	El-Ashraf Kāït-Bey	Mosque of Kāït-Bey, 1472
		Tomb-mosque of Kāït-Bey
		Mosque of Abū-Bekr ibn Mazhar, 1480
		Mosque of Kigmās, 1481
		Wekālas of Kāit-Bey
1496	En-Nāsir	Mosque of Ezbek El-Yūsufy, 1495
1498	Ez-Zāhir Kāusūh	
1500	El-Ashraf Gānbalāt	
1501	El-'Ādil Tūmān-Bey	
1501	El-Ashraf Kānsūh El-Ghūry	Mosque and tomb of El-Ghūry, 1503
1516	Tūmān-Bey	
1517	Egypt annexed by the 'Othmānly Sultān Selīm I of Turkey	

S. L.-P.

INTRODUCTION

ALTHOUGH the conquest of Egypt by the Saracens was completed in 641, we have no Arab monument, still standing in its original form, of an earlier date than 876. During these two hundred and thirty-five years of artistic silence, Egypt was merely a province administered by a succession of governors appointed by the Omayyad and 'Abbāsid Caliphs who had their seats at Damascus and Baghdād. The capital of Egypt was a provincial town, and no temporary governor, except its first conqueror,[1] cared to waste

---

[1] 'Amr's great mosque, founded at the conquest for the new capital called El-Fustāt, 'The Tent,' after the general's pavilion, has unfortunately so often fallen to ruin and been restored, that scarcely anything of the original building can be proved to remain; and it supplies no evidence for the history of Arab art. See E. K. Corbet Bey, 'The History of the Mosque of 'Amr,' in *Journ. R. Asiatic Society*, vol. xxii. N.S., 1891. The only other monument prior to 876 is the *mikyās* or nilometer at Rōda, which has a kufic inscription of the date of its restoration by the Caliph El-Mamūn when he visited Egypt in 217 A.H.=832 A.D.

upon it the wealth and labour necessary for great monuments. Where no monuments are built, Arab art cannot flourish: for to the Saracens architecture was *the* art *par excellence*, and all other branches of art were merely its handmaidens. Sculpture, painting, carving, inlaying, glass-work, were all cultivated mainly as auxiliaries to architecture. Hence, the period of mere governors is sterile not only in architecture but in the subsidiary arts, and but for a number of tombs discovered among the rubbish-mounds south of Cairo we should be without any early evidence as to the origin of the Arab style. The ornament, especially in woodcarving, of these tombs, however, shows beyond doubt that in the first centuries of the Hijra the Byzantine decorative manner prevailed in Egypt among Arabs, as among Copts; though as time went on the Muslims gave it a new development which made their architecture and all their arts individual expressions of their genius.

In 868 Ahmad ibn Tūlūn, the son of a Turkish slave of Bokhārā in the service of the Caliph El-Mamūn, was appointed governor of Egypt, and in the following year he declared himself an independent ruler. With him begins the history of Egypt as a distinct Mohammadan Power, and his mosque—which was but one of the many splendid, but alas! vanished, buildings with which he adorned his new *faubourg* 'El-Katā'i,'

CALIPHS

TŪLŪNIDS

N.E. of Fustāt—inaugurates the history of Saracenic architecture in Egypt. The mosque of Ibn-Tūlūn, built in 876—878, is familiar to every visitor to Cairo. Its great court surrounded by cloisters, with deeper rows of arches at the east or Mecca side (*līwān*), is a type of the earlier plan of Cairo mosques —a plan which was copied for centuries, even after other plans had come into vogue. The whole building is of plastered brick, except the curious corkscrew tower which, with some later additions, is of faced stone.¹ The massive piers are ornamented with engaged columns, the bases of which are imitations of ancient models. The capitals are campanulate, and the decorative foliage bears some relation to the acanthus. These and other details, such as the wavy pattern of the bordering of the arches, the mosaic plateband above the prayer-niche (*mihrāb*), etc., point to the dominating influence of Byzantine models, and identical ornament may be seen in some of the early tomb-carvings referred to above. On

---

¹ The only minaret standing, of the two originally placed at either end of the *līwān* wall, is of brick. The large stone tower in masonry and various architectural details appear to belong to a different period from the rest of the mosque. [Its remarkable resemblance, however, to one other monument, and one only, the corkscrew tower of Samarrā, built during the Caliphs' residence there in the IIIrd c. of the Hijra, justifies the belief that there was an original tower of the same form. See the woodcut of the Samarrā tower in Rich's *Kurdistan*, vol. ii., p. 151.—*Ed.*]

the other hand, on the intrados of some of the arches, where the original ornament is still preserved, we find already in the IXth century polygonal designs mixed with true arabesques, which are not Byzantine at all, but typically Saracenic.

The Tūlūnid dynasty, despite the promise of its birth, withered away in 36 years. A succession of thirteen governors for the Caliph again reduced Egypt for 30 years to the subordinate position of a province; and though the Ikhshīdid dynasty maintained its independence in Egypt and Syria for 36 years more, its princes never found the settled peace and leisure necessary for the undertaking of artistic monuments; even their tombs were at Damascus. There is not a vestige of any art during this interval.

FĀTIMIDS But in 969 Gōhar, the general of the Fātimid Caliph El-Muʻizz of Kayrawān, conquered Egypt, and with the accession of the new dynasty Egypt took its place as the most powerful oriental State on the Mediterranean. The Fātimids had already been great builders at Kayrawān, Mahdīya, and in Sicily: they did not abandon the taste when they transferred their capital to the new site of *El-Kāhira*, 'the Victorious,' italianated into *Cairo*, which they founded immediately after the conquest. El-Kāhira was originally no city but only the new Caliphs' vast fortress-palace—or rather pair of palaces—surrounded by the houses of their officers and slaves, and enclosed with massive walls. The palaces have long vanished, but some of the gates of the walls remain in the places where they were built by Bedr El-Gemály for the Caliph El-Mustansir in 1087: they are the Norman-looking Bāb-en-Nasr and Bāb-el-Futūh, close to the Arab Museum, and the Bāb-Zuweyla in the Sukariya. Of the mosques of the Fātimid period (969—1171) there still remain the great university mosque El-Azhar ('the Splendid'), the mosque of El-Hākim (in the court of which the Museum has its temporary asylum), the small mosque El-Akmar, and that of Talāi' ibn Ruzzīk, vezīr of the last Fātimid Caliph. Of these the oldest is the Azhar (971), but it has been so often restored that its original features are considerably obscured. The keel-form of the arches is characteristic of Fātimid work, though we find the pointed form on the next mosque, the ruined El-Hākim (990—1012), which in this and many other respects (e.g. carvings on wooden ties of piers, and of the door, see below, Passage No. 1) resembles the style of Ibn-Tūlūn. The mosque of Talāi' ibn Ruzzīk (1159) near the Bāb-Zuweyla, shows a marked advance in decoration. The simple arabesques of El-Hākim's inscriptional friezes have here developed into rich detail which gives the effect of filigree-work. Indeed the art of arabesque ornament as seen in the ruins of this beautiful mosque has reached a perfection which is not surpassed by any later decoration in Cairo. The mosque El-Akmar in the Sūk-en-Nahhāsīn built by the Caliph El-Āmir in 1125, small and ruined as it is, has the feature, unique among Fātimid mosques, of a fine façade (unfortunately hidden by a formless erection which the Monuments Commission has vainly sought to obtain power to remove) very unlike the ordinary plain exterior of the early mosques, and deserving special notice for the shell ornament of its fluted niche, the rosette of open tracery composed of inscriptions and ornament, and the side niches, surmounted by a kufic frieze. Moreover, the angle of this mosque shows the earliest example of that mode of stalactite transition which afterwards became a chief characteristic of Saracenic architecture in Egypt.

The last Fātimid Caliph was deposed by Saladin (Salāh-ed-dīn Yūsuf ibn Ayyūb), who founded the dynasty of the Ayyūbids (1172—1250), fortified the citadel of Cairo, built his palace there (no longer existing), and enlarged the circuit of the city walls. The influence of the Crusaders, who had covered Syria with fortresses, and with whom Saladin was constantly at war, may be traced in the military architecture of his dynasty. Another influence was the return of the Government of Egypt from the Shī'ism of the Fātimids to orthodox Sunnism. In order to encourage orthodoxy, the Ayyūbids founded a number of theological colleges (*medresa*), in which the religion of Islām, as taught by the Four Doctors, was systematically expounded.

AYYŪBIDS

These *medresas* are really mosques, with an open court in the centre, and a prayer-niche (*mihrāb*), pulpit, etc. in the eastern *līwān* or sanctuary at the side towards Mecca; but instead of cloisters round the court, the sanctuary and the three other sides are formed by arched transepts or porches, open to the court, which give a cruciform appearance to the building. In these four porches, divines expounded respectively the Shāfi'ite, Mālikite, Hanafite, and Hanbalite systems of Mohammadan theology. This cruciform plan afterwards became usual for small mosques, as well as for medresas, though the older cloistered form was still preserved for the great congregational mosques (*gāmi'*) used for Friday prayers.[1]

The oldest *medresa* still in existence[2] is that of El-Kāmil, the nephew of Saladin, built in 1224, but now an utter ruin, where only the plan can just be traced. Some remains of the decoration are in the Museum (Room I, nos. 83—87) and serve as com-

---

[1] In El-Makrīzy's *Khitat*, or 'Topography of Cairo,' etc., the distinction between the *gāmi'* (congregational mosque), *mesgid* (small mosque), *medresa*, etc., is carefully observed, and so it was when Lane wrote his *Modern Egyptians*, 1836; but in the present day the people of Cairo call any sort of mosque a *gāmi'*, or, roughly, *gama*.

[2] The earliest medresa, the Nāsirīya, founded by Saladin near the mosque of 'Amr, where the Shāfi'ite doctrine was taught, has disappeared.

plement to those of Talāi'. The college of Es-Sālih, 1242, and adjoining mosque, are also ruins, but some characteristic details remain: e.g. the façade with shell-ornament like El-Akmar, new stalactite forms, especially in the minaret (part of which, however, is restored), toothed borders, etc. Great progress had been made in the construction of domes, the angles of which were masked by a series of niches, as may be seen in the adjoining tomb of Es-Sālih (1249) and that of the Imām Esh-Shāfi'y (1211). In the former one traces western influences, especially in the introduction of a false gorge sculptured with foilage, in the entablature of the façade. The wood-carvings of the tomb show a greater delicacy than anything we have of the Fātimid period (even the beams of Talāi'), and it is much to be regretted that we have no monuments between the two by which we could trace the growth of this branch of art, which was cultivated with peculiar success in Egypt. The sober marble panelling of Es-Sālih's tomb also deserves notice, as contrasting with the more elaborate dados of a later epoch.

With the Mamlūk Sultāns of the Bahry or Turkish dynasty (1250—1382) we enter upon the richest and most flourishing period of Saracenic art and architecture. 'The Mamlūks offer the most singular contrasts of any series of princes in the world. A band of

MAMLŪK SULTANS

lawless adventurers, slaves in origin, butchers by choice, turbulent, bloodthirsty, and too often treacherous, these slave kings had a keen appreciation for the arts, which would have done credit to the most civilized ruler that ever sat on a constitutional throne. Their morals were indifferent, their conduct violent and unscrupulous, yet they show in their buildings, their decoration, their dress, and their furniture, a taste and refinement which it would be hard to parallel in western countries even in the present aesthetic age. It is one of the most singular facts in Eastern history, that wherever these rude Tartars penetrated, there they inspired a fresh and vivid enthusiasm for art. It was the Tartar Ibn-Tūlūn who built the first example of the true Saracenic mosque at Cairo; it was the line of Mamlūk Sultāns, all Turkish or Circassian slaves, who filled Cairo with the most beautiful and abundant monuments that any city can show.'[1]

There was a transitional period, at first, before the true Mamlūk architectural style was formed. In the mouldings of the great mosque of Ez-Zāhir Beybars (1268), the façades of Kalāūn's monuments, etc., we have signs of exotic influences; whilst the Gothic portal from a church at Acre, bodily transported to form the doorway of the medresa of En-Nāsir in the Sūk-en-Nahhāsīn, shows alike an appreciation of

[1] Lane-Poole, *Cairo*, pp. 95—97.

foreign styles and an indifference to artistic consistency. But these exotic influences from Syria and elsewhere soon found their true place and became assimilated, so far as they were harmonious, in the rapidly developing Mamlūk style. The long reign of over forty years (1299—1341) of En-Nāsir Mohammad, son of Kalāūn, gave time for the work of selection, adaptation, and precision, to which the admirable style of the numerous mosques erected by by En-Nāsir, his sons, and the officers of his court, bears witness. The abounding energy of this productive epoch bore the happiest results for art. The hesitating experiments of the earlier period gave place to a rare distinctness of architectural conception. Despite a remarkable variety and incomparable wealth of form and combination, the unity of design stands clearly out and reveals a finished and singularly adequate style.

In the arrangement of the façade, which is now of freestone, generally in two shades, the materials of previous centuries are developed and emphasized; the larger surfaces are given perspective by a system of high shallow niches in which the windows are set in double rows; these niches are brought back to the face above by stalactite cornices, and the portals, though wider and deeper, are treated in the same way and richly coated with marble. A long inscriptional frieze spreads across the façade, and the top is crowned by a crenellated moulding. The general plan of the mosque is the same as in previous periods, sometimes of the cloistered type with marble columns, but more commonly cruciform; but a new importance is given to the founder's tomb, always covered by a dome, which is, indeed, the characteristic mark of a tomb-mosque.[1] The spring of the arches round the court is set higher than before. The joists of the wood roof are magnificently carved, painted, and gilt. The wainscots or dado are of marble mosaic, often to the height of several yards, and the pavements are tessellated in bold and striking mosaics. The rich and harmonious effect of the interior is enhanced by the panelled and inlaid pulpit (*minbar*), lectern (*kursy el-kahf*), bronze lanterns, and enamelled glass lamps. And, from the few remains that have come down to us, none unfortunately at all complete, it is clear that the palaces and private houses of the Mamlūk age hardly fell short of the mosques in the beauty and elaboration of their form and decoration.

The accession of the Burgy or Circassian line of Mamlūks (1382—1517) introduced no fresh element of importance in the architecture, which continued its natural development without interruption or external interference. The mosques in the fifteenth century are more and more restricted to the cruciform plan and become smaller, which allowed the

---

[1] Lane-Poole, *Art of the Saracens in Egypt*, p. 60.

central court to be covered in. A number of secondary institutions were added to the mosque and filled up the spaces between its porches and the streets,—such as theological colleges, public fountains (*sebīl*), elementary schools (*kuttāb*), lavatories, and rooms for the mosque attendants. The school is an almost universal feature of Circassian Mamlūk mosques, and occupies as a rule one of the most conspicuous angles of the building, where its gracefully arched window may be seen high up. It first occurs in this position in the mosque of El-Gāy el-Yūsufy (1372). The founder's tomb was also given greater prominence. Instead of being relegated to a corner of the mosque, as under most of the Bahry Mamlūks, it is often the principal feature, or commonly forms a separate and complete monument. Stone was more generally employed, even for internal walls, which no less than the façade were covered with arabesques, geometrical designs, and kufic inscriptions, every inch of which is worthy of study. As the mosques of this period are smaller and more decorated than before, so the private houses are more *coquettes*. The *mak'ad* on its two arches overhangs the court, and the *kā'a* or salon is adorned with mosaics and a richly gilt and painted ceiling, softly lighted by the graceful *meshrebīya* lattice. Many *wekālas* (*khāns* or caravanserais), fountains, etc., like those of Kāït-Bey, are monuments of rare artistic merit. External decoration reached its highest point of elaboration under the Circassian Mamlūks.

When Egypt became in 1517 a province of the Ottoman Empire, its art took wings and departed. The 'Othmānlis imported the form of the Byzantine church, and gave a new importance to the dome, but brought no real artistic inspiration. Among the Turkish mosques may be mentioned that of Suleymān Pasha (1523), near the tomb of the saint Sāriyat-el-Gebel in the Citadel, and those of Sinān Pasha at Būlāk (1571) and Malika Safiya (1610). A few mosques were still erected by Egyptians more or less after the Mamlūk style; but the tendency was in favour of buildings of less importance, such as fountains, schools, caravanserais, and darwīsh convents. The *sebīls* of the Turkish period especially form a notable feature in the streets, and are independent buildings, no longer subordinate to mosques. Ornament suffered an eclipse; the rich decoration of Kāït-Bey gave place to a simple and cheap manner significant of artistic and pecuniary poverty. An exception is seen in the buildings and restorations of the admirable 'Abd-er-Rahmān Kikhya (properly Ketkhuda), whose fountain, for example (1744), is chiefly in the Arab style and stands far above all contemporary Turkish work, which is generally beneath contempt. It is devoutly to be wished that the political and industrial revival which was inaugurated by the illustrious founder of the present dynasty, the great Mohammad 'Aly, may find its corollary in a renaissance of that artistic fertility which was once among the glories of Muslim Egypt.

HERZ

CATALOGUE

OF THE

NATIONAL MUSEUM OF ARAB ART

ROOM I.

Stucco, Stone, and Marble Work

Stucco was used in the Arab art of Egypt from the earliest times as a material for architectural ornament. We find examples in the oldest extant Mohammadan monument, the mosque of Ibn-Tūlūn, built in A.D. 876-8, which, in spite of its thorough restoration in 1296, retains a portion of its original stucco decoration. In the XIIIth century stucco reached its highest perfection in Cairo, when the tomb of Kalāūn and the *medresa* or collegiate mosque of his son En-Nāsir (1299) furnish admirable examples of profuse decoration in this material. The stucco ornaments nos. 83-87, however, are of an earlier date, for they formed part of the framing of a window of the long-ruined mosque of the Ayyūbid Sultān El-Kāmil, nephew of Saladin, which was built in 1224, and of which, according to the late James Wild, two sides were still standing in 1845 and displayed ornament which resembled that of the Alhambra.¹ These fragments, nos. 83-87, show us how the plaster was worked. We see at once that the design was cut in the solid block and that the decoration is in two distinct planes: the ornament of the first plane was finished first, and then the parts in relief were added in a second layer. Stucco decoration was used at all periods, even when sculptured stone held the first place: compare the kufic frieze of the stateliest of Cairo mosques, that of Sultān Hasan (1358), and the beautiful ornament of the dome of Aksunkur (1347) in the Darb-el-Ahmar. In the second half of the XVth century stucco was less popular than stone, but the Kubbet el-Fidāwīya in the suburb of 'Abbāsīya, which belongs to this period, shows, by the profuse stucco ornamentation of the whole of the interior to the very apex of the dome, that the art had not been lost or degraded, and that the method of cutting out the designs was the same as in earlier times.

Stucco was also used for filling in windows, in two ways: the first and more ancient is the *claire-voie* or open tracery window cut out of a thick layer of plaster, often with very happy effect, in a great variety of designs. This method was used until the close of the XIIIth century. Examples

---

[1] Lane-Poole, *Art of the Saracens*, p. 53. There is no doubt that the internal decoration of the tomb-mosque of Kalāūn and a window in the south arcades of the mosque of El-Muayyad bear a striking resemblance to Moorish ornament.

may be seen in the mosques of Ibn-Tūlūn[1] and El-Hākim, and the ruined but magnificent mosque of Ez-Zāhir Beybars, where remains of richly designed tracery still stand out here and there in the roughly blocked-up bays. The Māristān (hospital) of Kalāūn has also some fine and well-preserved gratings of cut plaster. This kind was used to fill the window-bays of mosques of the cloistered style; or, when mosques were entirely closed-in (as the Māristān or those of Kāït-Bey etc.) they served to protect the glazed windows proper, which were inside. These glazed windows (*kamarīya* 'moonlights' or *shemsīya* 'sunlights') are not found before the second half of the XIIIth c., and are of two kinds. In the earlier kind (say 1250-1330), after the design was cut in the plaster, the pieces of thick coloured glass were laid on the face so as to cover the holes, and were fixed in their places by little rims of plaster which followed the lines of the pattern. Examples may be seen at the tombs of Es-Sālih and Kalāūn and the sepulchral mosque of Sengar el-Gāwaly (1323). In the later style of *kamarīya*, of the XIVth and XVth c., the little rims are omitted, and the glass is fixed to the back of the stucco by pouring a coat of liquid plaster between the pieces of glass. There are examples in the medresa of Barkūk in the Sūk-en-Nahhāsīn (1384), in buildings of the epoch of Kāït-

---

[1] Probably not of the date of the foundation, but of the restoration in 1296: they are too bold and decided to belong to the earlier date; but they undoubtedly replaced older stucco gratings.

Bey (end of XVth c.), the mosques of Abū-Bekr ibn Mazhar, Kigmās el-Ishāky, etc. The glass of these later windows is sometimes extremely thin. The *kamarīya* of recent centuries will not bear comparison with the older specimens : the designs become poor, the execution coarse, and the colours (which had then to be imported, for lack of local materials) thin and inharmonious.

Freestone was not generally employed by the Saracenic architects of Egypt, in place of brick or rubble, till a rather late date, notwithstanding the examples set before their eyes in the stone buildings of the ancient Egyptians. It is true that the Palace of the Fātimid Caliph El-Mu'izz, begun in 970, is stated to have had walls constructed of stones ' so well joined that one would think they were made in a single block,'[1] and the three city gates, the Bāb-el-Futūh, Bāb-en-Nasr, and Bāb-Zuweyla (1087-91) are splendid examples of stone masonry; but all the mosques up to the XIIth c. are built of brick.[2] The first stone mosque is that called El-Akmar,[3] in the Sūk-en-Nahhāsīn, built in 1125 by the Fātimid Caliph El-Amir; and here only the façade is of stone,

---

[1] Nāsir-i-Khusrau (A.D. 1040), *Sefer Nameh*, transl. Ch. Schefer, p. 129.

[2] The stone base of the dome in the court of Ibn-Tūlūn's mosque dates only from the restoration by Lāgīn in 1296, as its inscription states. So do, in all probability, the minaret and the adjacent cloister, which are also of stone.

[3] See the 6th Annual Report of the Commission for the Preservation of the Monuments of Arab Art, 67th rapport, where I have given a plan of the mosque El-Akmar.

the arches inside are of brick resting on marble columns. But the stone-work is admirably executed, the shaping accurate, the joining exact, and the sculpture of ornament and inscription very skilful. Evidently this was not a first attempt, though it is the earliest known to us. It leads the way for a series of similar buildings with stone façades and brick interiors, which prevailed till nearly the end of the XIIIth c., when brick was generally abandoned in favour of stone, laid with wide joints, and roughened to receive the mortar.

Before 1330 bricks were almost exclusively used for minarets. The sumptuous monument of Kalāūn, which combined mosque, tomb, and hospital, furnishes the first example of a stone tower.[1] Thenceforward stone minarets increased until they became almost universal under the Circassian Mamlūks, when stone was everywhere the favourite material for all parts of buildings, and it becomes evident that the architect has mastered the most difficult problems of construction. This development of constructive skill came to its perfection in time to assist the decorative spirit of the Circassian period, and exquisite arabesques admirably executed in stone are lavished upon the monuments. At the same time the dome, which had hitherto been coated with stucco, a frail material for ornament, is also constructed of stone,

---

[1] El-Makrīzy says that the minaret of Akbughā (1331) was the first to be built in stone, *after that of Kalāūn.*—*Khitat,* ii., p. 384.

and becomes a subject for elaborate decoration. The earliest stone domes, those of the tomb-mosque (1405-1410) of Barkūk, the first Circassian Mamlūk, in the Eastern Cemetery, are ornamented with zigzags. Immediately afterwards other domes are covered with graceful arabesques, which make one forget the hard material out of which they airily spring.

Presently, different coloured stones began to be chosen to aid in decoration, and by such variegation a sort of large mosaic was formed over a considerable part of the edifice, and eventually, not the gateways only, but the entire façade was treated in this fashion.[1] The first mosque, we believe, in which strata of different coloured stone were employed, was that of Ez-Zāhir Beybars, where the gateways are of stone of two alternating colours.

Stone was not used merely in construction, but also for tombs, pulpits (*minbar*), tribunes (*dikka*), etc., of which no more exquisite example can be cited than the *minbar* of white gritstone with which Kāït-Bey endowed the tomb-mosque of Barkūk; it is a perfect gem of Arab ornament.

Egypt possesses a considerable variety of stones suitable for building,[2] but the Arabs, instead of

---

[1] The vile practice of distempering the walls and façades of mosques in red and white stripes is a coarse attempt to revive the effect of varied stone courses. Every effort is being made by the Commission to suppress this crude imitation.

[2] See the collection in the School of Medicine at Cairo.

going to the trouble of extracting their own materials from the quarries, preferred to rob the buildings of their predecessors; one often sees hieroglyphics on an outer wall of a mosque, whilst columns, capitals, lintels, etc., from demolished Graeco-Roman buildings, abound. The stone used in the best Arab period is a white limestone, of a close substance, which takes a greyish tone with age; or else a yellowish nummulite stone, too porous for the finest sculpture. The latter has been almost exclusively employed during the Turkish period.

Marble was used at all periods by the Arabs, but especially in the early days of their occupation of Egypt for tombstones (*shāhid*), many of which, engraved (sometimes in relief) with pious formulas, the name of the deceased, and the date of death, in kufic characters, have been found in the sandy tract about 'Ayn es-Sīra to the south of Cairo. They date chiefly from the IXth c., but some go back earlier. A great many ancient tombstones have also been brought from the old Mohammadan cemetery near Aswān. Egypt is poor in marble, and the backs of these headstones often show that they were taken from older Greek, Roman, or Coptic monuments. Such spoliation was very common : we find a Roman eagle on a capital in the Citadel mosque of En-Nāsir, a cross and crown on another in the mosque of El-Muayyad, and Byzantine columns on either side of the niche (*mihrāb*) of the mosque of Ibn-Tūlūn—though this prince put himself to great pains to procure original materials and generally eschewed spoliation on principle. Others were less scrupulous, and cargoes of marble were brought from ruined cities of Syria, whilst the gothic gateway of the medresa of En-Nâsir, in the Sûk-en-Nahhâsîn, was ravished from Acre in 1291 by Khalîl. This habit of spoliation was injurious to the growth of Arab style, especially as to columns, which were generally borrowed; and, except the vase-shaped capitals (called *kulla*, after the earthen water-bottles of the same name), no true Arab capital appears till the characteristic stalactite form was introduced at a late date.[1] Marble was not generally employed till the XIIIth c., when it began to be used for veneering, especially on portals. When sculptured the work is naturally finer than on coarser stone; but the most beautiful decorative effects in marble are seen in mural mosaics and tesselated pavements. The *mosaics* were either formed of pieces of coloured marbles set in a mortar bed, or various small pieces were inlaid in the solid slab which formed the groundwork. When the outlines of the space to be inlaid were too complicated to be filled without needless labour in cutting the marble, the designs were filled in with a resinous composition, generally red or black. Many magnificent examples of mosaic may be seen in the mosques.

The Museum possesses a fine series of richly sculptured marble vessels (nos. 34, 35, 110, etc.).

---

[1] The earliest occur in the Medresa of Barkûk, 1384.

STUCCO, STONE, AND MARBLE WORK

Room I.
1. Marble slab inscribed 'In the name of God the Compassionate, the Merciful.' L 0·53¹
2. Marble slab, inscribed with name of God in relief. L 0·16
3. Grey marble fragment, with *kalima* 'There is no deity but God' in relief. H 0·34
4. Portion of marble slab, inscribed and originally painted. (From a tomb.) H 0·18
5, 6. Fragments of white marble tombstones with kufic inscriptions. (From cemetery of Imâm Esh-Shâfi'y.) H 0·58, 0·52
7, 8. Limestone inscribed with kufic characters. (Mosque of El-Hâkim, circ. A.D. 1000.) W 0·35
9. Marble slab. L 0·35
10. Marble medallion commemorating foundation of a mosque in 817 A.H. (1414). D 0·26
11. Marble slab, inscribed with name of Ahmad es-Sabt and date 1181 A.H. (A.D. 1767. Mosque of Sinân Pasha at Būlâk). L 0·63
12. Marble fragment of tombstone with kufic inscription. (Cemetery of Esh-Shâfi'y.) H 0·38
13. Marble slab with inscription and ornaments in relief. L 0·32
14. Fragment of marble tombstone inscribed with kufic characters. (Cem. of Esh-Shâfi'y.) L 0·27
15. Marble fragment with naskhy inscription. L 0·22
16. Marble slab of a fountain (*selsebil*),² sculptured. H 1·35

---

¹ The dimensions are given in mètres and centimètres. D = diameter, H = height, L = length, W = width. The mosques, streets, etc., mentioned are in Cairo, unless otherwise stated. Dates are A.D. unless stated to be A.H. The colour of marble is white unless otherwise described.

² Such slabs were set in the public street-fountains to cool the water which flowed over them.

ROOM I.
17. Part of a sculptured and painted marble slab. L 0·28
18. Sculptured marble slab, with traces of colour. (Mosque of El-Māridāny, 1338.) L 0·69
19. Sculptured slab from a prayer-niche (*mihrāb*), representing a hanging lamp (inscribed 'God is the Light of the Heavens and the Earth'[1]) between two candles, on an arabesque ground. (Medresa El-Budeyrīya, in the Sālihīya quarter, 1357.) H 0·61
20. Fragment of grey marble border; the sunk ornaments were formerly filled with resinous paste. L 0·70
21. Fragment of marble border. L 0·70
22. Angle of framing in sculptured greyish marble. L 0·16
23. Two marble octagonal shafts of columns from a *mihrāb*, sculptured on alternate faces with geometrical and foliate designs. (x c.) H 1·82, 2·00
24. Two conglomerate shafts of *mihrāb* columns, cut in facets. (Mosque of Haydar Shawīsh at Mansūra.) H 2·00
25, 26. Marble border, with symmetrical designs, incrusted with red and black resinous paste. (Fountain of Kāït-Bey in the Salība quarter, end of xv c.) L 0·65, 0·34
27, 28. Fragments of marble incrusted with red and black stone. L 0·30, 0·24
29, 30. Fragments of marble sculptured with ornaments originally coated with stucco. L 0·22
31. Marble slab of a street fountain, with arabesque ornament and border of finely sculptured animals. (Street-fountain, *sebīl*, of Farag in front of the Bāb-Zuweyla: beginning of xv c.) H 1·81

---

[1] Korān xxiv, 36. See below, p. 37.

I. 19. SLAB FROM A PRAYER-NICHE. XIVTH CENTURY

UNIV.
CALIF.

STUCCO, STONE, AND MARBLE WORK

Room I.

32. Marble stand for jar, sculptured with ornaments, nearly effaced. (Mosque of Kāit-Bey, 1472). L 0·55
33. Marble stand for jar, made out of the base of a column, resting on four feet, and covered with kufic inscriptions and ornaments. (Mosque of 'Saghry Wardy' (Taghry Berdy) in the Salība, 1440.) L 0·35

I. 34. MARBLE JAR PLACED ON
108. MARBLE STAND

34. Two-handled marble jar covered with arabesques, kufic inscription on neck, fish on base.

12 CATALOGUE OF THE ARAB MUSEUM

Room I.
(Medresa of El-Higāzīya, daughter of En-Nāsir. xiv c.)[1] H(inside) 0·70
35. Two-handled marble jar, ribbed. (Mosque of Umm-el-Ghulām, 1254.) H(inside) 0·70
36. Fragment of marble border, with gilt ornament. L 0·68
37. Slab of grey marble covered with arabesques. H 1·34
38. Mouth of a well formed of a marble Byzantine capital. (Mosque of Zeyn-ed-dīn, in the Darb-el-Gemāmīz.) H 0·30
39. Tombstone (*shāhid*) inscribed with name of Nabīl Bey and date 1235 A.H. (1819). H 0·98
40. Two serpentine columns of a *miḥrāb*, with ribbed shafts, and a cross cut on the capital. (Mosque of Kūsūn es-Sāky, now almost destroyed, 1329.) H 2·50
41. Marble tombstone with kufic inscription stating that it was erected by order of El-Hāfiz-li-dīni-llāh (the Fātimid caliph, 1130-1149). H 0·82
42. Marble slab inscribed with name El-Kawāmy El-Husāmy. (Hōsh el-Wāly, in cem. of Esh-Shāfi'y.) L 0·73
43. Limestone front of a tomb, with ornaments, and date 809 A.H. (1406). L 0·90
44. Tombstone of reddish sandstone inscribed with kufic characters. (x c.) H 0·44
45. Corner of limestone coving, sculptured with foliage surrounding a spread eagle. (Possibly of the Fātimid epoch. Found in the quarter of the Bāb-esh-Sha'rīya.) L 0·95
46. Fragment of marble with naskhy inscription. L 0·43

---

[1] According to Prisse d'Avennes, these jars were reserved in the mosques for the religious ablutions of special personages.

Room I.

47—50. Serpentine tombstones with kufic inscriptions, dated 465, 459, 589, 429 A.H. (A.D. 1037-1193. From Kôs, in Upper Egypt.) H 0·47, 0·60, 0·60, 0·70

51—53. Diorite tombstones, inscribed, and dated 443 (1051), 590 (1194), 567 (1171); no. 52 in naskhy, the others in kufic. H 0·90, 0·72, 0·85

54. Mural mosaic of red and black stone, mother-of-pearl, and turquoise enamel. (Mosque of Kûsûn, 1329.)

55, 56. Marble Byzantine capitals, one sculptured with cross. (Mosque of Kûsûn, 1329.) H 0·34, 0·31

57. Marble slab sculptured with arabesques. L 0·51

58, 59. Marble fragments from a tomb. Modern.

60, 61. Marble Byzantine capital. (Mosque of Kûsûn, 1329.) H 0·40

62. Marble tombstone inscribed in kufic with name of Hasan ibn Hoseyn and date 462 A.H. (1069). H 0·64

63. Marble base of a column, sculptured. (Mosque of Murád Pasha.) H 0·40

64. Marble tombstone with kufic inscription dated 262 A.H. (875). H 0·68

65, 66. Two Corinthian capitals (one side plain) in reddish stone, with traces of gilding. (Mosque of Kûsûn, 1329.) H 0·38

67, 68. Red and green porphyry, from a dado. L 0·34, 0·31

69. Black stone inlaid with characters in white marble. L 0·36

70. Fragment of marble tombstone, with kufic inscription, dated at the end of iii c. A.H. L 0·38

71, 72. Slabs of marble engraved with armorial bearings, a spread eagle, and a goblet. (Bath of Aïsha el-Hammâmîya in the Darb-el-Gemâmîz, now demolished.) L 0·46

ROOM I.
73—75. Keystones in black and red stone and white marble. L 0·10
76. Marble vase, open-work. H 0·23
77, 78. Fragments of inscribed marble. L 0·13, 0·25
79. White stone, shaped to resemble three plates joined together. (From débris in mosque of Ibn-Tūlūn, 876-8.) L 0·30
80. Fragment of marble slab with kufic inscription commemorating the foundation of the mosque of Ibn-Tūlūn in 876 A.D.[1] L 0·27
81. Marble slab with kufic inscription. L 0·20
82. Sculptured marble. (Mosque of El-Māridāny, 1338.) L 0·12
83—87. Five stucco fragments carved with kufic letters. (Framing of window in ruined medresa of El-Kāmil, 1224.)
88. Marble fragment with kufic inscription, xvi c. L 0·27
89. Piece of mural mosaic in white marble and black, red, and yellow stone. H 0·29
90. Portion of marble slab with kufic inscription. (Cemetery of 'Amr at Masr el-'Atīka.) L 0·29
91. Fragment of veined marble. L 0·19
92. Fragment of sculptured marble. L 0·18
93. Cast bronze octagonal lantern (*tannūr*) for 110 lamps, in open-work, chased with ornaments and inscriptions, giving name of Sultān Hasan. (Mosque of Sultān Hasan, 1358.) H 2·00
94. Three coloured glass and stucco window-lights (*kamarīya*). Modern. H 0·92

---

[1] Another similar piece is now fixed in the *līwān* or sanctuary of the mosque, where it was found during repairs five years ago.

Room I.
95. Part of marble frieze sculptured with ornaments. xviii c.   L 0·22
96. Three coloured glass window-lights. (Demolished cupola near the tomb of the Imām Esh-Shāfi'y.)   L 0·32
97. Limestone bas-relief, a lion clutching a gazelle. (Modern.)   L 0·75
98. Marble stand for jar, with four feet, sculptured with ornaments, mythical animals, and kufic inscription.   H 0·47
99. Inscribed marble slab. (Given by M. Pugioli.)   L 0·45
100. Marble tombstone with kufic inscription in relief.   H 0·67
101. Dark syenite tombstone with naskhy inscription, in form of a *mihrāb*, giving name of Sheykh Abu-l-Hoseyn 'Aly ibn Absa, and date of death 637 A.H. (1239), with name of sculptor—'Made by Mohammad ibn el-Hāgg Ahmad.'   H 0·59
102. Curved piece of limestone, carved with floral ornament, on a gilt ground.   H 0·34
103. Serpentine tombstone of Ya'kūb ibn Ibrāhīm el-Marāzy.   L 0·22
104. Marble fragment with kufic inscriptions on both sides. (Given by Dr. Schweinfurth.)   L 0·68
105. Limestone vase with four heads of geese. (Modern; given by Dr. Schweinfurth.)   D 0·15
106. Plate in limestone. (Modern; given by Dr. Schweinfurth.)   D 0·15
107. Marble stand (*kelya*), sculptured with ornaments and kufic inscription. (Mosque of Makla-Bey Tāz.)   H 0·44
108. Marble stand ornamented with mythical animals with human faces, etc. (Mosque of Zeyn-ed-dīn, in the Darb-el-Gemāmīz.)   H 0·43

ROOM I.
109. Marble stand, on four feet, with kufic inscr. in relief (nearly obliterated), and engaged pilasters at the sides. H 0·42
110. Marble jar. (Mosque of Saghry Wardy.) H 0·60
111. Marble jar, with grey veins. (Zāwiya of Seyf-el-Yazal.) H 0·60
112. Marble centre of fountain, with kufic inscriptions on sides. D 0·49
113, 114. Angle of a tomb, engraved with ornaments and kufic and naskhy inscriptions richly sculptured. H 0·92
115, 116. Marble shafts of columns. (Niche of *sebil* of Kaït-Bey, near El-Azhar. End of xv c.) H 1·69, 0·69
117, 118. Bases of preceding. H 0·19
119. Limestone sundial. L 0·59
120. Marble sundial, dated 1163 A.H. (1749). L 0·95
121. Marble slab engraved with kufic inscr. on one side, and naskhy on the other. W 0·50
122. Coloured glass and stucco window. (Modern.) H 0·89
123. Marble Corinthian capital. H 0·39
124. Marble slab engraved with naskhy inscriptions. (Medresa of Barkūk, in the Sūk-en-Nahhāsīn.) L 0·30
125. Grey marble jar. H 0·66
126. Marble jar with three handles. H 0·66
127, 128. Two marble jars, inscribed 'Our lord the Sultān el-Melik el-Ashraf Abū-n-Nasr Kaït-Bey (exalted be his glory) bestowed this jar (*zīr*) for this blessed fountain on account of Mohammad and his family.' (End of xv c.) H 0·53, 0·61
129. Marble angle of a tomb with inscriptions and ornaments in relief. (Mosque of El-Chirkesy, in the Beyn-es-Siyārig.) H 0·86

STUCCO, STONE, AND MARBLE WORK

Room I.
130. Marble stand for jar, with two heads in relief on either side. H 0·43
131. Marble stand for jar, with kufic inscriptions and heads. H 0·42
132. Marble stand for jar, corners rounded. H 0·40
133. Marble stand for jar, in two pieces. H 0·41

ROOM II.

METAL-WORK[1]

In no department of Arab art is the influence of the style which the Persian Sasanians inherited and developed from Assyrian models more distinctly visible than in metal-work, where we find the Persian ornamentation by means of human and animal figures prevailing in spite of the objections of strict Muslims. The traveller Nāsir-i-Khusrau, who visited many Mohammadan countries in 1035-1042, besides noticing the gold and silver work at Tyre and Jerusalem, dwells especially on the triumphs of the goldsmith's art which he saw in Egypt in 1040. In the palace of the Fātimid caliphs at Cairo he saw the throne of El-Mustansir, which was made of pure gold and silver, chased with beautiful inscriptions and hunting scenes; and the inventory of the same caliph's possessions recorded by the historian El-Makrīzy describes an extraordinary collection of magnificent objects in the precious metals and stones. All these have disappeared, however, and it is only from the

---

[1] A fuller sketch of the history of this branch of art may be read in the French edition of this Catalogue.

close of the XIIIth c., that we are able to study Egyptian metal-work from objects still in existence; but thenceforward its development may be continuously observed up to the beginning of the XVIth c. The connection with Mesopotamia is easily traced. Many objects bear the name of the artist and of the city of Mōsul,[1] and we see the characteristic style of Mesopotamian ornament in the human figures, hunting scenes, etc., chased in silver, inlaid on bronze. The contemporaneous metal-work of Egypt itself reveals the same technical method of inlay and chasing, but the ornament is modified in accordance with the prevailing ideas of all Saracenic decoration in that country. There is more floral and geometrical ornament, of the same style that we see in woodcarvings and stone and stucco work of the period, and less of the representation of figures and animals which is typical of Mōsul.

Amongst the choicest examples in the Museum is the *kursy* or table (no. 13) of the Mamlūk Sultān En-Nāsir Mohammad, on which we see indeed representations of ducks (in allusion, no doubt, to the name of En-Nāsir's father Kalāūn, which means 'duck' in old Turkish),[2] but these figures are quite subordinate to the floral and geometrical decoration. This table is unquestionably a product of the Saracenic art of Egypt, and El-Makrīzy tells us[3] that

---

[1] See S. Lane-Poole, *The Art of the Saracens in Egypt*, pp. 151 ff.
[2] Idem, *ibid.*, p. 164.
[3] *Khitat*, ii., p. 105.

there was a 'Market of Inlayers' (Sūk-el-Keftīyīn) at Cairo, and that richly chased objects, such as a *dikka* or settle, inlaid with silver and gold, after the manner of our table, formed a prominent feature in wedding gifts. One of them belonging to Sitt-el-'Amāïm ('Lady of the Turbans'), a merchant's daughter, was so richly decorated that her betrothed gave her 100,000 *dirhems* (francs) merely to *repair* it. This passion for costly inlay had already vanished in El-Makrīzy's day (he died in 1441), and only a small number of inlayers then plied their trade.[1] The value which the owners placed upon such possessions may be inferred from the fact that they often had their names engraved upon them, and one sometimes finds a series of successive proprietors' names on a single dish or bowl.

The metals employed were copper and its various alloys, which can only be distinguished by chemical tests. The objects include large caldrons, coffers, tables, bowls, censers, candelabra, lamps, bosses and plating on doors, etc. The last are most readily dated and ascribed to Cairo workers, and some which have been found in the mosques are now in the Museum. The oldest are the folding doors (Annex I, no. 9) from the mosque of Es-Sālih Talāi' b. Ruzzīk, built A.H. 555 (1160), which are covered with starlike polygonal designs in cast bronze on a thin surface of brass.[2] Here the cast-

---

[1] S. Lane-Poole, *op. cit.*, pp. 165-167.
[2] The mosque, which still stands opposite the Bāb-Zuweyla, though in a ruined state, was restored after the

ings are plain; but others are engraved with very graceful designs, as on the doors which came from the medresa of Tatār el-Higāzīya, granddaughter of Kalāūn, founded in 761 A.H. (1359). To about the same time (1362) belongs the door of the tomb of Sultān Hasan, with its delicate inlay of gold and silver. The two leaves of the medresa of Barkūk, with bronze foliage coated with silver, and those of El-Ghūry, show that the art was still pursued with undiminished skill under the Circassian Mamlūks. The various lamps and lanterns or chandeliers in the Museum, of the XIVth c. and XVth c., are constructed in tiers to carry numerous little oil lamps, which were prevented from dripping upon the worshippers by a tray (like no. 107 in Room II) hung beneath, which also concealed the unattractive interior. The tray in question is partly in repoussé work, chased with decoration of the latest Mamlūk style; for it comes from the mosque of El-Ghūry, founded in 1503. The gratings, especially those which closed the windows of *sebīls* (street drinking-fountains), were also subjects for decoration, and their knobs were often engraved with the name of Allah or the arms of the founder; for heraldic devices were much in vogue in the XVth c. Nothing in the way of metal-work, however, surpasses for taste or skill the *kursis* already mentioned, or the little book-box (no. 57), with its delicate designs

---

earthquake of 1302 by Seyf-ed-dīn Bektemir; but the doors are of the Fātimid style, and must have belonged to the original building.

and enchanting kufic border, which still show traces of the gold inlay which was reserved for the finest class of work. After the XVIth c., bronze fell out of vogue; it was no longer used for the doors of mosques or other public buildings, and although gratings were still made of it, they were no longer skilfully fitted together, but were cast in a single piece. About the second half of the XVIIIth c., western influences begin to intrude in the designs.

Besides bronze, the Arab smith worked in iron. Nāsir-i-Khusrau mentions the iron-plated doors of the Haram at Jerusalem, and also the massive iron doors of El-Mahdīya in Tunis. In Egypt, iron was not in great demand for artistic purposes, but one may cite the forged iron gratings in certain mosques, especially in that of En-Nāsir in the Citadel, which attracted the attention of El-Makrīzy. Iron nails arranged in effective patterns were sometimes used to decorate the doors of mosques (see nos. 10, 50, in Passage) and some of the old gates of the city quarters, which were formerly closed at night.

Unfortunately, the Museum possesses no specimens of Saracenic arms or armour. There was once an Armourers' Market in the Beyn-el-Kasreyn, opposite where Kalāūn's tomb now stands. The present Armourers' Market (Sūk-es-Silāh) is near the mosque of Sultan Hasan, but it has not inherited the reputation of its predecessor.

11. 12. INLAID SILVER AND BRASS KURSY.   XIVTH CENTURY
[*To face* p. 23*

Room II.

1. Brass candlestick of mosque, engraved with inscriptions. (From the Citadel.) H 0·37
2. Brass candlestick, with traces of silver inlay, engraved with inscription in the name of the Mamlūk Sultān Husām-ed-dīn Lāgīn, who presented it to the mosque of Ibn-Tūlūn, when he restored it in 1296. H 0·41
3. Part of a copper vessel engraved with ornaments and inscriptions in name of a certain mamlūk of En-Nāsir. xiv c.? H 0·18
4. Covered vessel (lamp?) in copper, with repoussé ornament, and inscription in name of Sultān Hasan. (From his mosque, 1358.) H, with cover, 0·44
5. Base of a crescent, *hilāl* (formerly surmounting a dome), engraved with ornaments and inscriptions in praise of a Sultān. H 0·30
6. Upper part of a vase, edged with ornaments and inscriptions. (Medresa of Barkūk, 1384.) H 0·19
7. Part of a copper vessel engraved with ornaments and inscriptions bearing Mamlūk name. xiv c. H 0·33
8. Fragment of a copper vessel with ornaments and inscriptions. (Medresa of Barkūk.) H 0·14
9. Copper goblet-shaped vessel with ornaments and inscriptions. H 0·40
10. Cup (*tās*) engraved with verses. H 0·37
11. Brass vessel engraved with inscriptions. H 0·33
12. Brass *kursy* (table) of open-work, richly chased and inlaid with silver. (Medresa of En-Nāsir, 1299.) H 0·70
13. Brass *kursy*: the sides are divided into panels by borders of naskhy inscriptions in silver inlay in honour of Sultān En-Nāsir Mohammad; the panels are of filigree work, chased with

ROOM II.

arabesques and inscriptions partly inlaid with silver; in the centre of the top is a rosette formed by a kufic inscription, and in various places are representations of ducks in silver inlay; one of the panels forms a folding door through which a pan of live charcoal was doubtless introduced to keep the tray of food warm.[1]   xiv c. (Māristān of Kalāūn.)   H 0·82

14. Two fragments of brass plates, engraved with inscriptions (traces of silver inlay), with, on three sides, a frame of chased filigree work in copper, cast. (Tomb-mosque of Barkūk, 1405—1410.)   L 0·39, 0·41

15, 15A. Two pieces of cast-brass bordering from a door, fleur-de-lis filigree work.   L 0·24, 0·31

16. Brass tray of mosque lantern, in repoussé work, chased with animals and inscriptions. (Mosque of Sultān Hasan, 1358.)   D 0·75

17—20. Four brass plates engraved with ornaments. (Door of tomb-mosque of El-Ghūry, 1503.)   L 0·34, 0·27, 0·27, 0·34

21. Angle of brass panel with engraved and repoussé ornament.   L 0·24

22. Brass plate engraved with decorative interlaced kufic inscription on arabesque ground.   L 1·04

23. Fragment of brass plate with inscriptions giving name of En-Nāsir Mohammad.   xiv c.   L 0·21

24, 25. Two brass door-plates, engraved with ornaments and inscriptions in honour of a Sultān.   xv c.?   L 1·31

26—31. Six brass door-plates engraved with ornaments and inscriptions, commemorating the foundation of the mosque of Ezbek el-Yūsufy

---

[1] See S. Lane-Poole, *Art of the Saracens*, p. 189.

Ill. 57. Korán Case plated with Brass inlaid with Silver and Gold. [*To face* p. 25

ROOM II.

Ras-nawbat-en-nawâb (commander of the royal guard), A.H. 900 (1495), still standing in the quarter of the Birket-el-Fîl. L 0·85, 0·86, 0·69, 0·84, 0·39, 0·70

32—48. Seventeen chased brass door-plates. (From the xv c. mosque, at right of the Musky, but now demolished, of Ezbek ibn Tutush [not to be confounded with Ezbek el-Yûsufy above mentioned], who was Atâbeg el-Asâkir or commander-in-chief, and gave his name to the Ezbekîya quarter.) L 0·65, 0·61, 1·35, 0·70, 0·54, 1·28, 1·16, 1·30, 1·02, 1·00, 0·64, 0·58, 0·58, 0·64, 0·15, 0·46, 0·46. (No. 45 retains some of its nail-heads.)

49, 50. Two brass squares in chased filigree work, from a door. L 0·13

51—53. Three pieces of squares like preceding. L 0·13, 0·44, 0·44

54, 55. Two cast-brass knockers engraved with ornaments. L 0·34

56. Iron lance found in the mosque of El-Ghûry. L 0·70

57. Korân-case of wood, plated with brass, richly chased and inlaid with silver and traces of gold on a ground of black paste; the inscriptions give neither name nor date. (Tomb-mosque of El-Ghûry, 1503.) L 0·44, H 0·28

58. Wooden lock (dabba) plated with chased and repoussé silver. (Tomb of Seyyid 'Abd-el-Âl, at Tanta.) L 0·21

59. Wooden lock, similar to preceding. (From Mansûra.) L 0·17

60. Wooden lock, plated with silver, with repoussé ornaments and inscriptions. (Mosque of Seyyida Zeyneb.) L 0·26

61, 62. Two silver gilt balls engraved with name of 'Othmânly Sultân Mustafâ ibn Mohammad and

Room II.
dated 1032 A.H. (1623). (Tomb of Seyyid El-Bedawy at Tanta.) D 0·24
63, 64. Brass ewers coated with mother-of-pearl. H 0·18
65. Three silver anklets (*khulkhāl*). (From a tomb in Upper Egypt.)
66. Twenty-four iron arrows, found in the wooden roofing of the Ghūrīya street. (When this roofing was removed in 1882 the beams and planks were found to be riddled with arrows.)
67. Coins (four gold) found during the demolition of houses in the Ghūrīya.
68. Lower part of a brass crescent engraved with Mamlūk inscriptions and ornaments. H 0·20
69. Upper part of a copper vessel engraved with Mamlūk inscriptions, ornaments, and medallions containing heraldic arms, a lozenge. H 0·20
70. Turban-support from a tomb, copper. (Tomb of Seyyid El-Bedawy at Tanta.) H 0·22
71. Copper plate with repoussé inscriptions bearing name of Sultān Lāgīn. (From a door near the *mihrāb* of the Mosque of Ibn-Tūlūn, restored by Lāgīn in 1296.) L 1·40
72. Copper coins found in a demolished house in the Ghūrīya.
73. Two cast and turned brass candlesticks. H 0·44
74. Two turned wooden candlesticks with plates of tin: rude work. H 0·35
75, 76. Cast-brass candlestick. H 0·21, 0·38
77. Cast-brass candlestick with perforated tray. H 0·55
78. Part of cast-brass lamp. D 0·20
79. Cast-brass candlestick with perforated tray. H 0·41
80. Upper part of a four-branched brass candlestick. H 0·25

Room II.
81. Brass suspenders for oil-lamps (four of the lower eight missing).
82. Tin suspender for 20 branches of oil-lamps.
83, 84. Copper tray with four candlesticks. D 0·34
85. Brass tray with three candlesticks. L 0·26
86. Twenty-one cast and perforated brass trays (and two pieces) for suspension of oil-lamps, in two patterns. D 0·46
87. Three turned cast-brass students' lamps. H 0·72 —0·78
88. Brass filigree lamps. (Mosque of Seyyid El-Bedawy at Tanta.) D 0·22
89. Five cast-brass cups from a street fountain. H 0·11
90. Six cast-brass cups with inscriptions in name of the 'Othmānly Sultān Mahmūd I and dated 1164 A.H. (1750). (Sebīl of Sultān Mustafā III, built in 1760, opposite the mosque of Seyyida Zeyneb.) H 0·13
91. Two knockers of cast-brass filigree work. L 0·23
92. Brass knocker, richly chased. D 0·23
93. Brass anvil of knocker. H 0·11
94. Brass knocker, perforated and chased with ornaments, with traces of armorial bearings in central disc. L 0·25
95, 96. Lattice-work of brass wire from a window. D 0·72
97. Shield with iron centre-plate. (Mosque of El-Ghūry, 1503.) D 0·47
98. Fifteen brass chains for suspending lamps.
99—101. Upper parts of copper crescents. H 1·63, 0·65, 0·80
102, 103. Copper crescent (traces of gilding on 103). H 0·71, 0·80
104, 105. Parts of copper crescents. H 0·53, 0·36

Room II.
106. Brass crescent with plates engraved with inscriptions on both sides. (Mosque of Sultān Hasan, 1358.) H 0·34
107. Brass lantern of 160 lights with four turrets, and tray below, in open and repoussé work, engraved with ornaments and inscriptions. (Medresa of El-Ghūry, 1503.) H 2·60
108. Brass lantern, for seven lights; upper part dome-shaped, engraved with inscriptions. (Mosque of Seyyida Zeynab, 1760.) D 0·38
109. Brass lantern, like preceding, but dome of open work. (Mosque of Seyyid El-Bedawy at Tanta.) D 0·32
110. Brass lantern, shaped like hexagonal cone, for seven lights, and nine branches, engraved with ornaments, and inscriptions in the name of Kigmās Amīr-Akhūr (Master of the Horse, to Kāït-Bey), whose arms appear on a medallion in the centre of each side: on a fess, a cup inscribed with hieroglyphic characters, supported on either side by a cornucopiae; in chief, a lozenge; in base, a small cup. (Probably from mosque of Kigmās, built 886 A.H., 1481, at the entrance of the Darb-el-Ahmar, and now in process of restoration.) H 1·10
111. Copper tray of lantern, with medallions containing inscription in honour of a Sultān.
112. Eight pieces of perforated and chased cast-bronze. (Doors of Medresa of Barkūk, 1384.) L 0·24—0·60
113. Copper vessel (lamp?) with three handles. H 0·41
114. Two pieces of copper plating of a casket, chased with ornaments and inscriptions and inlaid with gold and silver. (Medresa of Barkūk.) L 0·33

Room II.
115. Tongue of iron lock. (Medresa of Barkûk.) L 0·85
116. Ten stucco and coloured glass window-lights. (Modern.) H 0·52—1·55
117. Brass tray of lantern engraved with inscriptions and ornaments. D 0·78
118. Cast-brass candlestick. H 0·63
119. Iron tongs. (Mosque of El-Ghûry.) L 0·34
120. Copper octagonal lantern with perforated brass sides, for eight lights. L 0·34

ROOM III.

GLASS

THE earliest specimens of Arab glass are the little discs used for weights (found in great numbers in the rubbish-mounds round Cairo), of which dated specimens exist from the first century of the Hijra.[1] Nāsir-i-Khusrau mentions a 'Market of Lamps' (Sūk-el-Kanādīl) close to the Mosque of 'Amr, and refers to the admirable glass-work of Egypt.[2] No. 1 in Room III, which we owe to Dr. Fouquet, the well-known Cairo physician, illustrates the varieties of beads and enamel found in the Cairo mounds. But the chief glory of Arab glass-work in Egypt is represented by the collection of over sixty enamelled glass lamps in the Museum, which, despite air-bubbles, bear witness to the skill of the artists in the variety of the decoration, the grace of the inscriptions, the finish of the work, and the colouring of the enamels. These glass lamps are always of

---

[1] See S. Lane-Poole, *Catalogue of Arabic Glass Weights in the British Museum*, and P. Casanova, *Catalogue des pièces de verre de la Collection Fouquet, Mem. miss. arch.*, Tome vi., 1893.

[2] *Sefer Nameh*, p. 152.

the same shape (see pp. 35, 38, 42); a small oil-vessel was hung inside by wires hooked to the rim; and the lamp was suspended by silver or brass chains. The pure Arab style of decoration and the accurate calligraphy of the Arabic inscriptions leave no doubt that these lamps were made by native artists in Egypt; though in Turkish times, when indigenous art had decayed, it is possible that lamps w ere imported from Murano. The oldest lamp in the Museum, of which the date may be approximately fixed, is no. 12, of the XIIIth century,[1] and the most recent is no. 80, of the XVth century; but the collection is arranged, not in chronological order, but according to the system of decoration: indeed, so many lamps are without dates and come from buildings which afford no clue to the epoch of their manufacture, that an historical arrangement can hardly be attempted.

Reference has already been made (p. 3) to the stained glass set in stucco and used for windows in mosques and houses. The oldest still standing are those of the tomb of Es-Sālih Ayyūb, who died in 1248. These are of thick glass, like those of the XIVth century; but in the XVth century the coloured glass of similar windows is thinner than a millimètre. Red and blue were used in three

---

[1] This is, however, very exceptional. Most lamps do not date earlier than the xiv c. The Arabs call them *Kandīl Kalāūny*, 'Kalāūn's lamp,' which seems to show that they first came into vogue in that Sultān's reign, 1279-1290. *Ed.*

shades, green and yellow in two shades; the colour is not painted on with enamel, but always in the metal itself, which is full of air-bubbles like the metal of the lamps. Judging from the frequency of a rounded rim to the glass, it would seem that it was made in small sheets.

Glass was also sometimes used in little cubes (about 10 millimètres square) with a gilt face for mosaic-work. They were evidently cut in the soft out of larger sheets, for the edges are squeezed, but the gilt surface is always well preserved. So far this material for mosaic has been found only in the prayer-niches (*mihrābs*) of the mosques of Ibn-Tūlūn and of Akbughā (XIVth century, which forms part of El-Azhar). Turquoise-coloured vitreous enamel was much used in the XIVth century for the pilasters which decorate the wall in which the *mihrāb* is sunk.

A. SMALL OBJECTS

Room III.
1. Collection of 90 pieces, including beads, bits of enamel, and other glass objects, found in the rubbish-mounds south of Cairo,[1] and illustrating the methods and varieties of early Arab glass-work. (Presented by Dr. Fouquet, 1893.)

---

[1] These mounds, or rather low hills, consist of the rubbish-heaps of the city of Fustāt, the original capital of Mohammadan Egypt, which was burnt in 1168 to prevent its occupation by the Crusaders.

Room III.
2. Collection of 19 oil-lamps and phials, blown and cast, from the same mounds. (Presented by Dr. Fouquet, 1893.)
3. Two glass weights, and two imitation agates, from the same mounds.

B. Globes

4, 5. Green and blue glass globes, used for decorating the chains which support lamps. (Mosque of Ezbek el-Yūsufy, 1495.) H 0·18, 0·15
6. Fragment of oval enamelled glass globe, with two birds in a medallion (see lamp no. 62). (Given by Dr. Fouquet, 1893.)

C. Lamps without colour

7. Ball-shaped lamp with three ears. H 0·25
8. Lamp, six-eared. (Mosque of Sha'bān, 1368.) H 0·32
9. Lamp, three-eared. (Mosque of Sultān Ḥasan, 1358.) H 0·25
10. Lamp, six-eared, wavy. (Mosque of Sha'bān.) H 0·30
11. Lamp with six enamelled blue ears. H 0·24

D. Lamps with little Enamelled Ornament

12. Lamp of plain glass with inscriptions and ornaments in gold and red enamel, three ears, foot wanting: the historical inscription is مما عمل برسم التربة المباركة السلطانية الاشرفية الصالحية يغمر الله ساكنها بالرحمة والرضوان 'Of what was made for the blessed tomb of the noble Sultān Es-

D

ROOM III.

Sâlih,[1] God cover its indweller with compassion and favour.' xiii c.   H 021

13. Lamp with ornaments and inscriptions in panels separated by floral designs in blue enamel; six ears; historical inscription :— المـقـام الشـريـف الاعظم المولوى السلطانى الملكى الاشرفى ناصر الدنيا والدين شعبان 'His excellency, the noble, mighty [mamlūk] of the lord the Sultan El-Melik el-Ashraf Nāsir-ed-dunya wa-d-dīn Sha'bān.'[2] xiv c.   H 036

14. Lamp of plain glass decorated on neck after the manner of no. 13. The letters are drawn on the glass with a border of red lines, and the panels have a blue ground applied inside. The inscription between the ears is the same as on no. 13. xiv c. (Mosque of Sha'bān.)   H 032

15. Lamp, enamelled and ornamented on the neck; inscription on the body referring to Sha'bān, as before. xiv c. (Mosque of Sha'bān.)   H 036

16. Lamp of plain blue glass with armorial bearing, a cup, in red enamel; inscriptions and ornaments (apparently once gilt) almost effaced. (Medresa of Barkūk, 1384.)   H 028

17. Lamp of plain blue glass, with traces of gilt. (Mosque of Alty Barmak.)   H 028

E. LAMPS DECORATED WITH ENAMELLED FLOWERS

18. Lamp entirely covered with floral decoration on a blue enamel ground.   H 034

---

[1] The reference to the tomb of Es-Sālih and its inmate shows that the lamp must have been made after that Ayyūbid Sultan's death in 647 A.H. (1248); and it is hardly likely that his tomb would have been adorned with lamps by anyone later than the xiii c.

[2] El-Ashraf Sha'bān ruled 1363—1377; his mamlūk, the amīr who owned this lamp, would thus belong to the second half of the xiv c.

Room III.

19. Similar to preceding, but with traces of gilding; on the neck and body, medallions inscribed in honour of a Sultān.[1] (Mosque of Sultān Hasan, 1358.)

F. LAMPS COVERED WITH ENAMELLED ORNAMENT

20. Lamp covered with tracery in white, and ornaments in red, blue, green, and yellow enamel,

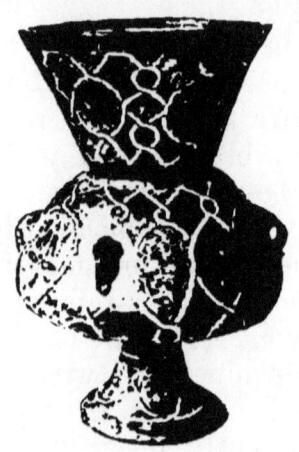

III. 20. ENAMELLED GLASS LAMP OF SULTĀN HASAN. XIVTH CENTURY

on a ground originally gilt; on the neck, three medallions containing rosettes; and three others with inscription in honour of a Sultān. (Mosque of Sultān Hasan, 1358.) H 0·42

---

[1] The delicate inscriptions in such medallions, which occur on the majority of lamps, are dedications to the Sultān, either with or without his name: those of Sultān Hasan do not mention the name, those of Barkūk do. They are often a mark of respect from some officer, and do not necessarily imply that the lamp or other object was actually made for the Sultān himself. See Herz, On the mosque of Ezbek El-Yūsufy, *Revue Égyptienne*, no. 1, Cairo, 1889.

ROOM III.
21. Lamp enamelled; above the six ears, medallions in the name of Ez-Zāhir Abū-Sa'īd [Barkūk]. (Medresa of Barkūk, 1384.) H 0·36
22. Lamp enamelled with blue border round the ears and rosettes on the body, with medallions on neck and body in name of Barkūk. (Medresa of Barkūk.) H 0·36
23. Lamp enamelled over body with network of blue, and flowers in red, blue, green, and yellow enamel; inscription in medallions in name of Barkūk. (Medresa of Barkūk.) H 0·36
24. Lamp enamelled with ornaments in various colours; a border of blue round the ears, which are separated by floral ornaments; six floral medallions on the neck; medallions on the body in name of Barkūk. (Medresa of Barkūk.) H 0·37
25. Lamp enamelled with arabesques on the neck, and medallions in name of Barkūk. (Medresa of Barkūk.) H 0·36; damaged.
26. Lamp enamelled with ornaments, geometrical patterns, and medallions in honour of a Sultān. (Mosque of Sultān Hasan, 1358.) H 0·45; foot replaced in wood.
27. Lamp nearly similar to preceding. (Mosque of Sultān Hasan.) H 0·40
28. Lamp similar to two preceding, but patterns more complex, and between the floral designs of the neck birds[1] delicately drawn within trefoils. (Mosque of Sultān Hasan.) H 0·40

G. LAMPS WITH INSCRIPTION ROUND THE NECK

29. Lamp with inscription on neck formed out of a ground of blue enamel: مما عمل برسم تربة لعبد

---

[1] Birds in flight are among the ornaments of several of these lamps.

Room III.

الفقير الى الله تعالى سيف الدين سلار نائب السلطنة المعظمة غفا الله عنه 'Of what was made for the tomb of the poor servant of God (exalted be He!) Seyf-ed-dīn Salār, viceroy of the exalted empire, whom God assoilzie.' (Salār was viceroy of Egypt from 1299 to 1309.) H 0·25

30. Lamp enamelled with ornaments, medallions inscribed with titles of Barkūk, in very delicate script; blue enamel border to the six ears; and on the neck on a blue ground an inscription (originally gilt) from the Korān, ch. xxiv, v. 36: 'God is the light of the heavens and the earth; his light is as a niche in which is a lamp, and the lamp in a glass,—the glass is as it were a glittering star.' H 0·37

31. Lamp enamelled with ornaments and medallions with titles of Barkūk, like preceding. (Medresa of Barkūk, 1384.) H 0·37

32. Lamp enamelled with floral ornaments, medallions in honour of a Sultān, and on the neck part of the verse from the Korān quoted under no. 30 in blue enamel decorated with white scrolls. (Mosque of Sultān Hasan, 1358.) H 0·41

33. Lamp very similar to preceding, with same inscription, but with blue enamel reticulation over the body. (Mosque of Sultān Hasan.) H 0·36

34. Lamp similar to preceding, same inscription with traces of gilt ground. (Mosque of Sultān Hasan.) H 0·41; foot broken.

35. Lamp with floral ornament on clear glass, and enamelled floral border round ears in red, blue, white, yellow, and green; inscription from Korān on neck, interrupted by medallions containing inscriptions in praise of a Sultan. (Mosque of Sultān Hasan.) H 0·35; foot wanting.

Room III.

36. Lamp with white enamel scrolls round inscription on neck, rosettes in several colours between ears, and neck inscription like no. 35. (Mosque of Sultān Ḥasan.) II 035

37. Lamp with ornaments between ears enclosed in white enamelled ornament; same verse from Korān. (Mosque of Sultān Hasan.) II 037; broken.

38. Lamp with body covered with blue enamel reticulation enclosing flowers; same Korān verse. (Mosque of Sultān Hasan.) H 038

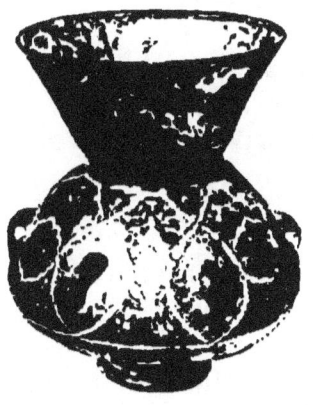

III. 38. Enamelled Glass Lamp. XIVth Century

39. Lamp with central belt of white enamel fleurs-de-lis, and ornaments; letters of Korān verse decorated with white scrolls. (Mosque of Sultān Hasan.) II 038

H. Lamps with Inscriptions on the Body

40. Lamp, with blue enamel interlaced decoration, relieved with red lines round the neck, and red-lined inscription round the body:—

عز لمولانا السلطان الملك الظاهر ابو سعيد نصر[ه] الله تعالى

ROOM III.
'Glory to our Lord the Sultān El-Melik ez-Zāhir Abū-Saʻīd [Barkūk], God (exalted be He!) aid him.' (Medresa of Barkūk, 1384.) H 0·39

41. Middle of a lamp like 40, from the same medresa.
H 0·16

42. Lamp enamelled with armorial bearings on neck and under body (on a fess, a lozenge), and inscription round the body: المقر الاشرف العالي الكافلي العلائي المرحوم. امير علي الماردانى
'His excellency, the most noble, exalted, protecting, El-ʻAlāy, the departed Amīr ʻAly El-Māridāny.' (Mosque of El-Māridāny, 1338.)
H 0·35

43. Lamp, enamelled, with inscriptions on medallions of neck and on body in honour of Ez-Zāhir [Barkūk]. (Medresa of Barkūk.) H 0·39

44. Lamp, enamelled, with inscription as preceding. (Medresa of Barkūk.) H 0·40

I. LAMPS WITH INSCRIPTIONS IN BLUE ENAMEL ON NECK, AND INSCRIPTIONS IN CLEAR GLASS ON BLUE ENAMEL GROUND ON THE BODY

45. Lamp with enamelled verse from Korān on neck, and inscriptions on body and in medallions in name of Barkūk. (Medresa of Barkūk, 1384.)
H 0·34

46, 47. Lamps resembling preceding. (Medresa of Barkūk.) H 0·34, 0·32

48. Neck of similar lamp, with name of Barkūk in medallions. (Medresa of Barkūk.) H 0·25

49. Lamp, enamelled, with inscription on body: عز مولانا السلطان الملك الناصر ناصر الدنيا والدين حسن بن محمد عز نصره 'Glory to our lord the Sultān El-Mqlik en-Nāsir Nāsir-ed-dunyā wa-d-dīn Hasan ibn Mohammad, magnified be his triumph.' (Mosque of Sultān Hasan, 1358.) H 0·39

ROOM III.

50—53. Lamps similar to 49, from the same mosque.
H 0·40, 0·34, 0·37, 0·41

51. Lamp enamelled with ornaments and Korān verse in blue on neck, and inscription in honour of Barkūk in clear glass on blue ground on body. H 0·30; foot and part of body wanting.

55. Neck of lamp with inscription in blue enamel. (Medresa of Barkūk.) D 0·23

56. Lamp enamelled with panels of arabesques on lower part. (Same.) H 0·38, parts missing.

57. Body of similar lamp. (Medresa of Barkūk.) H 0·23

58. Piece of lamp similar to preceding. (Same.) H 0·18

59. Neck of lamp with small inscription in blue enamel. (Same.) D 0·24

60. Lamp richly[1] gilt and ornamented with flowers and birds in red, white, blue, yellow and green enamel; medallions with arms, two polo sticks addorsed; and inscription in slender letters in blue enamel: [مما عمل المقر العالى السيفى الملكى] الناصرى ' Of what was made by his excellency, the exalted, Es-Seyfy el-Meliky en-Nāsiry' [i.e. an Amīr who was successively mamlūk of Seyf-ed-dīn Kalāūn and En-Nāsir Mohammad.] H 0·34

K. LAMPS WITH NECK INSCRIPTIONS IN BLUE ENAMEL ORNA-
MENTED WITH WHITE, AND CLEAR BODY INSCRIPTION
ON BLUE ENAMEL GROUND

61. Lamp enamelled with ornaments, bead borders and birds; Korān verse on neck, and on body

---

[1] The well-preserved gold on this lamp gives an idea of the rich effect such lamps must have originally produced.

Room III.

the inscription: عز لمولانا السلطان الملك الناصر ناصر الدنيا والدين محمد عز نصره 'Glory to our lord the Sultān El-Melik en-Nāsir Nāsir-ed-dunyā wa-d-din Mohammad, magnified be his triumph.' (Medresa of Mohammad En-Nāsir, 1299.) H 0·34

62. Lamp richly gilt and enamelled, with arms on neck and body—on a fess, a cup, including an ancient hieroglyphic cartouche,[1] base plain—belonging to the Amír Tughatemir, whose inscription runs round the body of the lamp: برسم المقر الشريف العالى المولوى المالكى المخدومى السيفى طغتمر الدوادار الملكى الصالحى 'By order of his excellency, the noble, exalted, [mamlūk] of the lord, the king, the master, Es-Seyfy Tughatemir, secretary of El-Melik es-Sālih.' Late xiv c. H 0·39; body damaged.

63—65. Lamps enamelled with ornaments and medallions and inscriptions in honour of Sultān Hasan. (From his mosque, 1358.) H 0·41, 0·38 (neck broken), 0·29 (neck wanting).

66—75. Lamps with inscriptions and delicately traced medallions in honour of Sultān Hasan. (From his mosque.) With high foot—H 0·42, 0·41, 0·41, 0·40, 0·40, 0·37 (foot broken). With short foot—H 0·36, 0·36, 0·36; much damaged, 0·26

76. Lamp enamelled with ornaments: six medallions bearing a cup on a fess; a verse from the Korān on neck; and on body برسم المقر الاشرف العالى المولوى\المخدومى السيفى شيخو الناصرى

---

[1] See Rogers in *Bulletin de l'Institut Egypt.* 1880; Lane-Poole, *Art of the Saracens*, pp. 195, 229.

Room III.

'By order of his excellency, the most noble, exalted, [mamlūk] of the lord, the master, Es-Seyfy, Sheykhū en-Nāsiry' (i.e. successively in the service of Seyf-ed-dīn Kalāūn and En-Nāsir Mohammad). xiv c. (Given by Rostovitz Bey, 1886.) II 036

77, 78. Lamps with gilt letters on blue enamel ground for neck inscription, and inscription on body, in white enamel, in honour of Sultān Hasan. (From his mosque.)

III. 76. ENAMELLED GLASS LAMP OF SHEYKHŪ. XIVTH CENTURY

79. Lamp enamelled in red, blue, white, and green, inscriptions decorated with scrolls in blue enamel; that on the body in honour of Sultān Hasan. (From his mosque.) II 037

80. Lamp with three medallions bearing arms, and interrupting Korān verse in white enamel on clear ground on neck, continued on body in clear letters on blue enamel ground; and with another inscription at junction of neck— مما

عمل برسم المقر الاشرف العالى السيفى قان باى

Room III.

الجركسى نظام الملك 'Of what was made by order of his excellency the most noble, exalted, Es-Seyfy Kān-Bey the Circassian, administrator of the kingdom.' (Mosque of Kān-Bey, 1441.) H 0·28

81. Lamp enamelled with elaborate flowers and an ill-formed inscription,[1] عز لمولانا المقام الشريف السلطان المالك الملك الاشرف ابو النصر قائتباى خالد الله ملكه 'Glory to our lord the stately, noble sultān, ruler, El-Melik El-Ashraf Abū-n-Nasr Kāït-Bey, God prolong his reign.' H 0·37
82. Lamp, enamelled, made by Brocard of Paris, bought 1886. H 0·34
83. Lamp ornamented with red, white, and gold lines; chain beads painted inside. H 0·25
84. Case containing fragments of enamelled glass lamps, with medallions inscribed in name of Barkūk. (Found at medresa of Barkūk during repairs of 1892.)
85. Case containing fragments of enamelled glass lamps:—
   (a) Pieces belonging to no. 74; (b) pieces with name of Barkūk; (c) pieces resembling nos.13—15; (d) pieces resembling 18 and 19. (Mosque of Sultān Hasan.)

---

[1] The contrast between this lamp and all the others is obvious at the first glance. The enamels are wanting in brilliancy, the ornaments are not Arab at all, and the Arabic letters are ungainly. The two bands decorated with palmettes, etc., beneath the neck, touch each other, and show lack of taste in the workman. One cannot believe that the art of glass-enamel was so degraded at a time so rich in other artistic work as the reign of Kāït-Bey, yet the alternative would seem to condemn this lamp as a later forgery.

TEXTS.

Nos. 86 to 129 in Room III consist of pious inscriptions, 'texts' from the Korān, the names of God, of the Prophet Mohammad, of the first Four Caliphs, or of dedicatory verses, written in elegant Arabic and Persian, such as devout Muslims often present for the decoration of mosques and tombs. Some (e.g. nos. 87, 91, 93, 105) are ornamented with a picture of the Kaaba at Mecca. A few are on leather (nos. 110, 129) and one on silk (106). Many are dated, but the dates all belong to the present and the last century. They are interesting for the history of Arabic and Persian calligraphy and illumination, but do not, of course, belong to the best periods.[1]

MISCELLANEOUS.

Room III.

130. Bronze lantern, octagonal, in three stages, the top and bottom stage of open work, the centre containing a bright copper band with inscription. (Mosque of Kādy 'Abd-el-Bāsit, 1419.) H 2·25

131, 132. Two bronze pyramidal lanterns chased with inscriptions and ornaments. (Mosque of the wife of Kāït-Bey in the Fayyūm.) H 1·45

133. Hexagonal wooden lantern, painted and gilt. (Mosque of Suleymān Pasha in the Citadel.) H 1·10

134. Six stucco and stained glass window-lights. H 0·60—1·27

---

[1] The names of the scribes and the nature of the inscriptions will be found in the French edition of the Catalogue; but they present little that is interesting.

Ill. 130. Bronze Lantern. 1419

To face p. 44

UNIV. OF
CALIFORNIA

ROOM IV.

Woodwork

EGYPT is naturally very poor in wood, but the trouble and expense of importation have not deterred its artists from employing this material largely and with remarkable skill in their architecture and minor arts. The dryness of the climate has contributed to the successful employment of wood for building purposes. The pillars of the mosque of Ibn-Tūlūn, which have stood for more than a thousand years, have wooden ties, and the oldest brick domes are stiffened by a complete framework of wood. The mosque of Ibn-Tūlūn has also a large frieze of wood carved with a portion of the Korān in kufic letters,[1] and its arcades were formerly covered by a wooden ceiling, a small portion of which the Commission for the Preservation of the Monuments was able to retain during the recent repair of the mosque, and of which the joists were then visible. These joists consisted of a trunk of a palm tree sawn in two, and faced on the three exposed

---

[1] Not, as has been supposed, the whole Korān. Corbet Bey, in his *Life and Works of Ibn-Tūlūn*, says the frieze does not contain more than one-seventeenth of the Korān. He is wrong, however, in stating that the letters of the inscription were "cut out in solid wood and fixed on to the board": they are carved on the board itself in relief.

sides with planks. The spaces between the joists were divided by cross-beams into shallow compartments. This kind of ceiling has been in use, with modifications and improvements, from the beginning of Saracenic architecture, through the finest periods, down to our own day. Another method was to ceil the joists across with boards; and a third, which has the richest effect, consisted of a ceiling of stalactites. In all three methods the ceilings were always painted and gilt, with ornamentation carved in the wood or applied in stucco. This roofing never rested directly upon the walls: there was always a transition—an aesthetic necessity—formed by arching, coving, stalactites, etc., which was treated with the same splendour of decoration as the ceiling itself, and presented the utmost possibilities of Arab art in finished perfection, in form, and in colouring. Such ceilings, of which some beautiful specimens have come down to us, were not reserved for religious buildings, but were also employed for private rooms, as the few remains of early palaces and houses—such as the palace of the Amīr Beshtāk (XIVth c.) in the Nahhāsīn, or the house of Gemāl-ed-dīn Ez-Zahaby (XVIIth c.) in the Ghūrīya quarter—abundantly prove. But nowhere was the art of wood-carving and decoration developed in greater perfection than in the making of doors, shutters, pulpits, Korān-lecterns, tables, settles, stools, etc., which form the principal objects of the limited furniture in use in Arab mosques and houses.

In the treatment of surfaces two leading methods

of decoration were employed, (1) an intricate panelled joinery, or (2) open turned work.

1. *Panelling*. In the very earliest examples we find a tendency to multiply the number of frames or borders, which gradually grew into a complicated composition of polygonal frames enclosing panels sometimes as small as a centimètre in superficies. Apart from their love of geometrical designs, the Arabs had a good reason for this minute subdivision of their panels, in the warping effects of a hot climate on large surfaces. The ornamenting of the faces of the panels and frames was effected by carvings, inlay, or paint. In the mosque of Ibn-Tūlūn we have some of the oldest specimens of Arab wood-carving, in the ceilings of the door-bays (no. 75 in the Passage: next in date observe the door no. 1 in the Passage). Here the carving is in the shape of volutes cut deep in the wood, recalling the foliate ornament of the Byzantine style; a resemblance still more obvious in the wood-carvings found in the tract of 'Ayn es-Sira, south of Cairo, which date from the early centuries of the Hijra. Apparently the same style of ornament prevailed up to the XIIth c.; but in the XIIIth c., we notice a deviation from traditional forms: the panels become smaller, the lines finer and more complex (see nos. 49 and 50 in Room IV, and no. 55 of Passage). The last is from the annex of the tomb of Es-Sālih Ayyūb (1249); and the tomb-covering itself is the first example we possess of a style which was already well developed. The little panels are formed into

hexagonal stars and delicately carved, and here appears the representation of fruit-stalks which are a common feature in XIIIth c. wood-carving (see nos. 32, 33, 62, in Room IV). The *mihrāb* or prayer niche from the chapel of Seyyida Rukeyya (no. 62), which belongs probably to the same century, deserves special notice for its characteristic ornamentation of stems branching out of a vase. Wood-carving reached its highest development in the XIVth c.—the century of greatest splendour in all Arab arts—especially during the reign of En-Nāsir Mohammad, and under the influence of that Sultān's family and the officers of his court. The use of various coloured woods and inlay, already observed in the tomb of Es-Sālih Ayyūb, became more frequent, until eventually almost the whole surface is inlayed. In the XVth c. ivory begins to be used for inlaying. Good effects were also obtained by carvings on solid planed planks (see no. 5 in the Passage).

Under the Turkish domination a rougher mode of woodwork was employed, but the little panels were still retained, though seldom carved, unless perhaps with a single inscription. Wood, ivory, tortoiseshell and mother-of-pearl inlay is characteristic of this epoch. In the Delta a special kind of woodwork was produced, in which the panel-work was imitated by grooving.

No. 54 in Room IV and no. 4 in the Passage should be noted for their rare representations of men and animals.

2. *Turnery*. *Meshrebīya* ('a place for drink')

properly means the little projecting bay, in a turned lattice window, in which a porous drinking-vessel (*kulla*) was placed to cool by evaporation; whence it came to mean the lattice window itself, and commonly in the present day any sort of turned lattice-work. Doubtless this kind of turning dates from very ancient times, and was done with the same primitive bow-lathe as nowadays, but the fragility of the work has permitted very few old examples to survive, and the earliest to which we can still point is the massive lattice railing which encloses the tomb of Kalāūn (1284). We do not find the true delicate meshrebīya work in this grating or in the pulpit set up by Lāgīn in 1296 in the mosque of Ibn-Tūlūn,[1] though the latter has a finer mesh and inlaid knobs. The true meshrebīya is first found in the mosque of El-Māridāny (1338), where the *līwān* or sanctuary is separated from the court by partitions showing, among other kinds of turnery, a system of hexagons connected by little cylinders. At the beginning of the XVth c. we have some fine examples of meshrebīya (e.g. the pulpit of El-Muayyad), and the art attained its highest perfection and variety of design at the time of Kāit-Bey (e.g. the panel with kufic inscription over the door of the pulpit of the mosque of Abū-Bekr ibn Mazhar). Meshrebīyas naturally were used principally in houses, where they kept out the indiscreet glances

---

[1] Of which there are some panels in the South Kensington Museum.

of passers-by, whilst admitting air and a subdued light and giving a sufficient outlook; but they contributed not a little to the disastrous conflagrations which used to be common in Cairo. European *persiennes* and *shīshas* have now almost wholly superseded the meshrebīya lattices of the past, which with their corbellings and cornices once formed a beautiful feature in the external decoration of the house. The varied forms and designs, inlayings and carvings, of meshrebīyas cannot be described, but may be seen in the Museum, as also the method of introducing inscriptions (e.g. Room VII, no. 29).

A different system of lattice-work, chiefly used in the Delta, consists in crossed laths fretted with geometrical designs, producing an excellent effect.

Ivory was used for filling panels of wood framework, when it was generally carved, and for inlay work, combined with ebony, tin, redwood, etc., in a fine mosaic put together and sawn off in thin veneer after the manner of Tunbridge work in England. In this form it was largely employed in the XVth c., for borders and even for entire surfaces of furniture (Room IV., nos. 57—60). Ivory does not often occur by itself, except in a few rare specimens in the museums of Europe.

Room IV.
1. Piece of wood, carved, with traces of gold and colour. (Ceiling of mosque of El-Māridāny, 1338.) L 2·50
2. Folding door, with turned panels at top and bottom, and joined panels inlaid with ivory in the middle. (From a house.) H 2·26

ROOM IV.
3. Shield carved with tughrā (monogram) of Sultān Mahmūd II of Turkey. Modern. (Mosque in Darb-el-Asfar.) L 0·66
4. Top of a table (*kursy*) of wood inlaid with mosaic of ebony, ivory, and tin. L 0·51
5. Box for mosque offerings, wood inlaid with ivory. L 0·62
6. Two ostrich eggs carved with inscriptions and ornaments. (Mosque of Seyyid El-Bedawy, at Tanta.) H 0·17
7. Two ivory tablets carved with ornaments and inscriptions commemorating the foundation of a medresa or collegiate mosque. (Mosque of Sha'bān, 1368.) L 0·36
8. Part of board inlaid with mosaic of ebony, ivory and tin. L 0·15
9. Camel-bone (part) with black inscription. (Given by M. Philip, 1887.) L 0·20
10. Horn. (Mosque of Seyyid El-Bedawy, Tanta.) L 0·41
11. Lock (*dabba*) of wood inlaid with mother-of-pearl. L 0·15
12. Reliquary of painted wood. (Mosque of the Hasaneyn, c. 1770.) L 0·70
13. Tablet of wood, with names of God, the Prophet, the first caliphs, and verses in gilt stucco. H 0·75
14. Six small panels carved with arabesques. L 0·11 — 0·22
15. Panel carved with inscription, a verse of the Korān, and date 1175 A.H. (1761). (From the Delta.) L 0·37
16. Panel carved with inscription: امر بانشا هذا المنبر المبارك مولانا السلطان الملك الظاهر محمد ابو سعيد جقمق عز نصره 'Ordered the making of this sacred pulpit our lord the Sultān El-Melik ez-Zāhir

ROOM IV.

Mohammad Abū-Saʻīd Gakmak, magnified be his triumph.' (Mosque of Gakmak, 1453.) L 0·45

17. Part of tomb, no. 21, with inscription in the name of Sheykh 'Aly El-Bakly, deceased 696 A.H. (1296). L 1·07

18. Commemorative tablet with inscription like no. 16. (Mosque of Gakmak.) L 0·45

19. Tablet commemorating the gift of a copy of the Korān and lectern by Kāït-Bey: وقف هذا المصحف الشريف والكرسى مولانا السلطان الملك الاشرف ابو النصر قائتباى عز نصره ' This Noble Book and the lectern, dedicated our lord the Sultān El-Melik el-Ashraf Abū-n-Nasr Kāït-Bey, magnified be his triumph!' Latter part of xv c. L 0·34

20. Part of commemorative tablet with inscriptions dated 874 A.H. = 1469. (Mosque of Gakmak.) L 0·44

21. Two fragments of a tomb in wood panelling, delicately carved with inscriptions and ornaments; another part is no. 17. (Mosque of Imām Esh-Shāfiʻy, 1211.) L 0·14

22. Folding doors of panel-work inlaid with ivory. (Mosque of Ezbek el-Yūsufy, 1495.) L 1·92

23. Folding doors of panel-work inlaid with ebony and ivory carved with arabesques. (Mosque of Ibn-el-Bakry, in the Hārat-el-Utūf, c. 1370.) L 1·71 (top panels wanting).

24. Tablet commemorating restoration of pulpit, &c. of mosque of Kādy Yahyā Zeyn-ed-dīn at Būlāk (now called Jāmiʻ-el-Mehkema) by Khawāja Mustafā in the reign of Kāït-Bey. Late xv c. L 0·76

25. Panel carved with ornaments. L 0·48

26. Panel of white wood carved and bordered with ebony. L 0·36

WOODWORK

Room IV.
27. Part of lintel of pulpit of mosque of el-Amawy at Asyūt, with kufic inscription : مولانا ....
'...our lord and master the Imām El-Mustansir-billah, commander of the faithful.' xi c. L 1·00 وسيدنا الإمام المستنصر بالله امير المؤمنين
28. Carved panel. L 0·35
29. Square carved panel. L 0·49
30. Portion of carved framing. L 0·60
31. Stalactite angle-piece, made of joined wood. L 1·15
32. Prayer-niche (*mihrāb*) of carved wood flanked by two pillars. (Mosque El-Azhar.¹) H 1·65
33. Prayer-niche (*mihrāb*) of carved wood in small panels, with kufic verse from the Korān. (Mosque of Sitta Nefīsa, rebuilt c. 1760.) H 1·92, signs of clumsy repairs.
34. Tablet carved with kufic inscription commemorating erection of a *mihrāb* in El-Azhar in 519 A.H.=1125, with name of Fātimid caliph El-Āmir bi-ahkāmi-llāh. (Mosque El-Azhar, probably belonging to no. 32.) L 1·22
35, 36. Carved and perforated panels. L 0·45, 0·49
37. Secret door in form of cupboard, with small panelled door in middle inlaid with ivory, and compartments all round for vases, &c. H 1·59
38. Two panels of wood with plain ivory centres edged with mosaic. L 0·07
39. Four panels of wood with mosaic centres edged with ivory. L 0·05

---

¹ This mihrāb and the tablet no. 34 were both in the Azhar, and, though not found together, it seems probable that they were once united. The use of the palm-tree for forming the hollow, the simple outlines, and restrained foliate ornament are signs of early style; and no. 34 bears the date 1125. See P. Ravaisse, '*Sur trois mihrābs en bois sculpté*,' in *Mem. de l'Inst. Egyptien*, 1889.

ROOM IV.
40. Fourteen panels of wood, some inlaid with ivory, some carved. L 003—011
41. Two small ivory panels inlaid with ebony, ivory, and redwood. L 004
42. Three panels of wood inlaid with ivory and ebony mosaic. L 008
43. Part of a door, with panel-work carved or inlaid with ivory. H 084
44. Three ivory panels carved with ornaments, and on the two larger panels this inscription: الملك الناصر ناصر الدنيا والدين 'El-Melik en-Nāsir, Nāsir-ed-dunyā wa-d-dīn.' xiv c. L 006
45. Four small carved panels of ivory. L 016
46. Six wood panels inlaid with plain ivory centres bordered with fillets. L 007—010
47. Joists of carved wood with iron rings for suspending lamps, etc. (Tomb-mosque of El-Ghūry, 1503.) L 39
48. Korān-case of wood carved and painted with arabesques inside and out, with inscription (inverted in front): برسم المصحف الشريف المعظم ... فهو السلطان المالك الملك الاشرف ابو النصر قانصوه الغوري خلد الله ملكه 'For the Noble Powerful Book ... the Sultān, Ruler, El-Melik el-Ashraf Abū-n-Nasr Kānsūh El-Ghūry, God perpetuate his rule.' c. 1503. L 079, wrongly put together.
49, 50. Three sides of a wooden tomb-casing, finely carved with rich and graceful ornaments and inscription giving name of Husn-ed-dīn Tālib b. Ya'kūb. 1216.[1] (Tomb of Sa'dāt et-Talba, near the mosque of Imām Esh-Shāfi'y.) L 180

---

[1] The fourth side, containing the date 613 A.H.=1216, is in the South Kensington Museum, and is reproduced on page 55. See Lane-Poole, *Art of the Saracens*, p. 122 and fig. 44. On the back are carved ornaments of a much earlier date, probably done for an older tomb of 304 A.H.=916.

IV. 59. KURSY OF INLAID IVORY AND EBONY

To face p. 55

Room IV.
51. Two panels carved with name and title of Barkūk. L 0·40
52. Three carved panels. Modern. (From the Delta.) L 0·32
53. Small carved panel. L 0·18
54. Panel of ceiling carved and painted with birds and human beings, one of whom drinks from a cup. (Māristān of Kalāūn, 1284.) L 0·39
55. Table (*kursy*) of six sides with carved or turned panels, and stalactite cornice. H 0·93 !

CARVED SIDE OF A SHEYKH'S TOMB. 1216 A.D.

56. Table (*kursy*) with ebony panels carved with arabesques and edged with ivory. (Mosque El-Azhar.) H 0·98; repaired.
57. Table of wood inlaid with mosaics of ivory, tin, ebony, etc. H 0·78
58. Table, similar mosaics. (Mosque of El-Ghūry.) H 1·11
59. Table, similar mosaics. (Mosque of Sha'bān, 1368.) H 1·17
60. Table, similar mosaics, with arched opening keyed with ebony and ivory, and with medallions on the springs bearing arms, on a fess a lozenge. H 0·72

Room IV.
61. Desk of wood veneered with mother-of-pearl. Syrian? II 100
62. Prayer-niche (*mihrāb*) of carved wood set in rectangular framework of small carved panels arranged in geometrical patterns; on the back and sides, some panels are carved with a vase from which rise stems bearing fruit and flowers. (Chapel of Seyyida Rukeyya, c. 1135.) II 210

IV. 64. PANELLED DOOR OF ASHRAFĪYA, 1423

63. Settle of turned wood. (House of Wakf El-Araby.) II 115
64. Leaves of a door of panelled wood inlaid with ivory and ebony. (Mosque of El-Ashraf, 1423.) II 198

IV. 62. Mihrāb of Seyyida Rukeyya. XIIIth century

To face p. 56

VII

Room IV.

65. Korān-case, six-sided, of wood covered inside and out with delicate mosaics, divided inside into three compartments, each with ten grooves, to hold the 30 *ajzā* or divisions of the Korān; the hinges are of bronze incrusted with silver and gold. (Mosque of Sha'bān.) L. 071

IV. 66. FILIGREE BRONZE LANTERN. XIVTH CENTURY

ROOM IV.
66. Octagonal lantern in filigree bronze, with fleur-de-lis lozenge in centre of geometrical designs; on the top, in hammered brass, a crescent. (Mosque of Suyurghātmish, 1356.) H 1·90
67. Nine stucco and stained glass window-lights. H 0·82—1·74
68, 69. Two boards, panelled in geometrical patterns, and carved. (Mosque of El-Muayyad, 1420.) H 1·90, 2·00
70. Wooden frieze, divided into panels with benedictory kufic inscriptions, separated by stars. L 1·36
71, 72. Boards carved with ornaments and kufic Korān inscriptions. L 1·55
73. Board covered with carved ornament and inscriptions. L 1·77
74. Part of a board painted with white letters on red ground. L 0·70
75. Board panelled and carved, with gilt fleur-de-lis carved in a medallion, verse from Korān painted in the larger panels, and painted borders. L 2·15
76. Board painted with ornaments, inscriptions, and patterns. L 1·72
77. Part of a painted board. L 1·50 (Nos. 73—77 are from the Mosque of El-Muayyad.)
78. Board carved with inscriptions on both sides, taken from the Korān, except the second line of the obverse, which commemorates the foundation of the tomb by Sultān Farag:—امر بانشا
هذه التربة المباركة مولانا السلطان الملك الناصر
الدنيا والدين ابو السعادات فرج بن برقوق نصره الله
تعالى (Tomb-mosque of Barkūk, 1405—1410.) L 1·63
79, 80. Portions of carved board. (Mosque of El-Muayyad.) L 0·70, 1·00

WOODWORK 59

ROOM IV.

81, 82. Carved boards from covering of a ceiling joist. (Mosque of El-Muayyad.) L 1·16
83—89. Seven panels carved with inscription in relief:— هذا ما اوقفه مولانا السلطان الملك الناصر فرج بن برقوق 'This was dedicated by our lord the Sultān El-Melik en-Nāsir Farag b. Barkūk.' (Tomb-mosque of Barkūk.) L 0·72
90. Carved board. L 1·80
91, 92. Friezes carved with sunk ornaments. (Mosque of El-Muayyad.) L 1·10, 1·23
93. Board carved with geometrical patterns.[1] L 2·05
94. Piece of a board carved with ornaments of the earliest period. (Tract of 'Ayn es-Sīra, south of Cairo.) L 0·57
95. Panel carved with inscription recording erection of tribune (*dikka*) in tomb-mosque of Barkūk by Sultān Kāït-Bey, and with medallion carved and inscribed in honour of Kāït-Bey, in three lines. (From the tribune referred to, late xv c.) L 2·43
96. Panel carved with inscription commemorating restoration (*tejdīd*) of the mosque El-Azhar by Kāït-Bey, xv c. (El-Azhar.) L 0·82
97. Carved piece. L 1·03
98. Board ornamented with symmetrical arabesques. L 1·42
99. Carved board with traces of gilding. L 1·79

---

[1] Nos. 68, 77, 79, 80, 91, 93 were found upon the ceiling of the līwān of the mosque of El-Muayyad during the repairs of 1889, but certainly did not belong originally to the mosque. They were apparently thrown over the ceiling to fill up holes, and may have come from some private house or palace, as their propitiatory inscriptions would lead us to suppose.

ROOM V.

WOODWORK, *continued.*

ROOM V.
1. Two leaves of door panelled, and carved with geometrical ornament on top and bottom panels. (Delta.) H 1·60
2. Cupboard, with frieze, doors, and base, constructed of small panels of carved hard wood, and ivory inlaid with mosaics; sides plain. (Mosque El-Azhar.) H 1·60
3. Front of panelled cupboard with two arches at top. H 1·74
4. Door of carved and turned panels. H 1·52
5. Six pieces of wood carved with floral ornaments. (Wekâla Sunbul.) L 0·80 – 1·31
6. Part of carved framing. L 0·60
7. Board carved with arabesques. L 0·57
8. Six carved boards. (Wekâla Sunbul.) L 0·55 – 1·54
9. Board carved with Korân verse. L 1·90
10, 11. Two carved and fretted panels. (Mosque El-Azhar.) L 0·69
12. Entablature of frame of a pulpit (*minbar*) of carved wood. L 0·68
13. Two panels of a door. L 0·35
14. Part of carved ceiling. L 0·42
15. Part of carved board, with inscription connecting it with a fountain (*sebîl*). L 1·35

Room V.
16. Two stalactite brackets, with appliqué work at base. (House of Wakf El-'Araby in the Gôdarīya.) II 1·60
17. Leaf of door, middle panel carved with geometrical designs. II 0·72
18. Part of pointed arch in wood, with ornaments carved on the springs. L 0·98
19. Folding door carved with inscription. (Mosque of Seyyid Ibrāhīm El-Burkawy at Desūk.) II 1·95
20. Folding door of panel-work ornamented with bronze. (Same mosque.) II 1·44
21. Oblong panel carved and fretted. (Mosque El-Azhar.) L 0·85
22. Three pieces of carved boards from facings of joists. (Wekāla Sunbul.) L 0·70—1·55
23. Carved board from ceiling. (Wekāla Sunbul.) L 1·06
24. Door of small carved panels in carved framing. (Khānkāh of Beybars el-Gāshenkīr, 1306.) II 2·40
25. Side of pulpit door carved and inlaid with ivory. II 1·76
26. Framework of a door, in small panel-work carved with fleurs-de-lis, and borders carved with animals. (Khānkāh of Beybars el-Gāshenkīr, 1306.) II 2·33
27. Side of a Korān-reader's chair, with commemorative inscription dated 746 A.H. = 1345. (Mosque El-Azhar.) II 1·05
28. Central panel of ceiling, carved and painted, and inscribed in three lines : | ابو النصر قائتباى
عز لـمـولانـا السـلـطـان الـمـلـك الاشرف | عـز نـصـره
Abū-n-Nasr Kāït-Bāy, Glory to our lord the Sultān El-Melik El-Ashraf, Magnified be his triumph ! (Sebīl of Kāït-Bey, late xv c.) W 1·67

Room V.
29. Joist carved in relief with inscription in honour of a sultān. L 2·85
30. Lintel of door carved with inscription in name of El-Melik El-'Azīz 'Othmān b. Yūsuf b. Ayyūb, date 574 A.H. = 1178.[1] (Desūk, Lower Egypt.) L 2·12
31. Door of small panel-work. (House of Wakf El-Kasr 'Aly, xviii c.) H 2·00
32. Korān-reader's chair, panelled, on turned feet. H 1·05, repaired.
33. Carved bracket (for supporting framework from which lamps were suspended in the dome. See Room IV, no. 47). H 1·22
34. Door with bronze plates and bosses. (Tomb of Seyyid Ibrāhīm at Desūk.) H 2·17
35. Palmwood joist faced with boards originally painted. (Mosque Wakf el-Tawāfiya.) L 4·20
36. Korān-reader's chair, of turned wood and panelling inlaid with mosaics. (Mosque of Kigmās El-Ishāky, 1481.) H 1·56
37. Facing board of a ceiling joist, carved and painted white or gilt on blue ground. (Mosque of El-Muayyad, 1420.) L 1·00
38. Support of globe surmounting pulpit. (Mosque of Kūsūn, 1329.) H 0·90
39. Panel with carved surfaces. (Mosque El-Azhar, probably date of Kāït-Bey's restoration.) L 0·55
40. Part of carved ceiling, painted and gilt. L 0·78
41. Star-shaped painted table, turned panels at sides. (Tomb-mosque of El-Ghūry, 1503.) H 0·50
42. Ten stucco and stained glass window-lights. H 0·95—1·14

---

[1] El-'Azīz was then only a governor under his father Saladin.

Room V.
43, 44. Cross-pieces of cupboard with panels inlaid with ivory. (Mosque El-Gohariya in N.E. angle of El-Azhar, 1440.) L. 1·00
45. Front of cupboard, with panels carved with arabesques and propitiatory inscriptions, and little arches cut out above. H 2·21
46. Lanterns of sheet brass richly chased, for 100 oil-lamps, with dedicating inscription. (Mosque El-Azhar.) H 1·80

[For other examples of woodwork, see Room VII, Passage, and Annex I.]

Room VI.

Pottery

The potter's art was assiduously cultivated in Egypt from very early times, and it was certainly not allowed to deteriorate during the Mohammadan period. To quote Nâsir-i-Khusrau again, the eleventh century traveller found that at Cairo all sorts of faïence were made, and some so thin and transparent that you could see your hand through it; whilst another kind had a metallic lustre, the shade of which changed according to the point of view.[1] The traditions of ancient Egypt and of Greek and Roman examples, and the influence of Persian ceramic art, all contributed to the variety and beauty of Arab pottery. Almost a history of the art could be traced by means of the numerous fragments, from the commonest domestic crockery to the finest decorative work, daily picked up among the rubbish mounds which mark the site of the old city of Fustât (near 'Old Cairo'), and whence connoisseurs, especially Dr. Fouquet of Cairo, have accumulated very interesting and beautiful collections. Sometimes these fragments have the baking cockspur still sticking to them (e.g. no. 145), a conclusive proof of native manufacture, to which may be added the numerous wasters found among the rubbish heaps. Among

[1] *Sefer Nameh*, trans. Ch. Schefer, p. 151.

the most interesting fragments are the many which exhibit inscriptions or armorial bearings, and thus enable us to arrive at their date. The arms are often the same as those found on metal-work, glass lamps etc., such as the lion, two-headed eagle, cup, lozenge, etc.; and a careful classification of these indications with reference to dated examples in other arts would go some way towards making a foundation for the history of medieval Arab pottery. Among these fragments some are glazed faïence, others are merely baked earthenware of a hard unglazed paste, often stamped with marks indicating probably the capacity of the vessel. The glazed faïence forms a rich series worthy of more careful study than it has hitherto received. As an entrepôt of commerce between East and West, Egypt naturally received influences from all sides, and there is no doubt that certain oft-repeated designs (see nos. 135 and 138) must be derived from China, whence also came the undoubtedly Chinese celadon or sea-green glaze which had a great attraction for Egyptian potters (see no. 144). This celadon ware, which was preserved in families from generation to generation, is known throughout Egypt by the name of *Ghūry*, which may be derived from the well-known Sultān of the beginning of the XVIth c. who built so many monuments and often employed faïence for their decoration.

The fragments of vases in which an opaque enamel formed the glaze often bear on the bottom an artist's signature, e.g. عمل المصرى 'made by El-Misry [the Cairene'], عمل المعلم 'made by the Master,'

عمل الشأمى 'made by Esh-Sha'my [the Syrian'], or عمال بن الشامى 'made by the son of Esh-Sha'my;' or such names as غيبى Gheyby, and غزال Ghazzāl.

The Arabs, unlike the Persians, made but a sparing use of wall-tiles in their decoration; but this is explained, no doubt, by their preference for marble, which was readily obtained in Egypt or near by, and which in the form of mosaic produced a richer effect than tiles could give. In this preference they followed the Romans. As a matter of fact the only monuments of Arab rule in Egypt which are decorated with tiles are the minarets of the mosque of En-Nāsir in the citadel (1318), the tomb of Tāshtemir the Cupbearer (1334), and the tomb called that of the Khawand Baraka, of about the same date, the last two in the Eastern Cemetery or so-called 'Tombs of the Caliphs.' In the minarets of En-Nāsir the tiles are of single colours, white, brown, and green, and cover up the roughly-hewn stones of the upper stage. The cupola of Tāshtemir has a band of green tiles in the drum. That known by the name of Khawand Baraka (though it is not her tomb) has on its cupola a course of tiles forming an inscription, the upper edge of which is emphasized by a shoulder crowned with merlons. The large white letters stand boldly out of the ground, which is of two shades of green, and set off by foliage in dark brown faïence. The *ensemble* of letters, foliage, etc., has the appearance of a mosaic of irregular joints, which may almost be compared to the effect of a cyclopean wall.

We have to skip a century and a half before we find another monument with this characteristic. The visitor to the Museum will be struck by the large plaques of tiles barred by great white letters on a blue ground. These letters are of unusual excellence, and formed on so large a scale that they cover two courses of tiles. The ornaments which fill up the intervals have the true Arab *cachet*. The registers state that they came from the tomb of El-Ghûry, and if they really belonged to it they probably formed a band round the dome, like those already mentioned. The present dome is a wooden erection set up by Franz Pasha, about fourteen years ago; but we learn from Prisse d'Avennes,[1] that the original dome, which was shaken by an earthquake and had to be demolished, was ornamented outside, first by squares of blue faïence, like the minaret [*scil.* the minaret of El-Ghûry's collegiate mosque, opposite the tomb-mosque which had no minaret], then by a band of inscription, and finally by little blue and white imitation windows fixed between the windows of the dome. Among a heap of waste sherds I found a piece of faïence, no. 328, which I have placed over no. 273, of which it is the complement in colour of glaze, ornaments, and character of inscription. These fragments apparently formed part of one of those commemorative tablets which in the XIV and XV cc. were often set up in the name of some Sultân; and in this case the Sultân's name

---

[1] *L'Art Arabe*, p. 123.

is El-Ghūry. This and other evidence makes it clear that in the tiles mentioned above, and notably those of the tomb of El-Ghūry, we see a native manufacture. It should be noticed that only one or two colours are used in these Egyptian tiles. It was only when Egypt came under 'Othmānly rule that tiles became fashionable for architectural decoration, on the walls of mosques, houses, and especially the combined street-fountain (*sebīl*) and school (*kuttāb*) which is a prominent object in Turkish building. The mosque of Aksunkur (1347) restored in 1652 by Ibrāhīm Aga Mustahfazān, and the mosque of the Amīr Sheykhū (1355), have sometimes been cited as examples of the early use of wall-tiles: but a glance at the latter will show that the tiles are mixed up without any method with the remains of the original marble mosaic work, and there is no doubt that the tiles which line the *līwān* of Aksunkur were placed there by the restorer Ibrāhīm Āga. The tiles of both mosques, too, are not of the simple Arab style; they are Turkish— Prisse d'Avennes classed them conveniently [but we know not on what authority] as Kutahia ware. Of course, in time Egypt learned to manufacture tiles in the Turkish style, yet with an individual character— e.g. at Rosetta; but the art has long fallen into decay (witness the mihrāb of the mosque of Sitta Nefisa at Cairo dated 1171 A.H. = 1757), the kilns burnt out, and in the present century imported tiles from Italy (see no. 252) have been employed in decoration.

A. Unglazed Earthenware

Room VI.
1. Cup. D 0·17
2. Cup. D 0·15
3. Cup. (Mosque of El-Ghûry.) D 0·14
4. Cup, with signs of glaze inside. D 0·11
5. Tall vessel. H 0·15
6. Small vessel. H 0·04
7—9. Water-jars. (Mosque of El-Ghûry.) H 0·08—0·12
10, 11. Lamps. H 0·13, 0·12
12, 13. Pipes. H 0·03
14. Brick. (Masr el-'Atîka.) L 0·15
15, 16. Greek fire grenades, stamped with name Mohammad. H 0·11
17—34. Eighteen fragments of vessels with various marks. (Given by Dr. Fouquet.)
35. Vessel in shape of quadruped. (Given by Dr. Fouquet.) L 0·14
36. Jug with ovoid base. H 0·37
37, 38. Amphoras with pointed base. (Mosque of Imâm Esh-Shâfi'y.) H 0·55, 0·60
39. Jug with spherical base. H 0·37
40. Jug with flattened base. H 0·21
41. Talisman (*higâb*) with stamped inscriptions. D 0·06

B. Glazed Pottery

42—59. Eighteen lamps. L 0·09—0·12
60. Globe for lamp-chain, of terra cotta with yellow enamel. (Mosque of wife of Kâit-Bây in the Fayyûm.) D 0·11
61, 62. Globes of glazed pottery with blue flowers on white ground. D 0·22
63. Bottom of dish, white enamel, blue and black ornament, inscription outside. (Mosque of El-Ghûry.)
64. Dish with moulded border in various colours. D 0·38

Room VI.
65. Piece of a plate with inscription. D 0·20
66. Lamp, coloured decoration on opaque white ground, inscription from Korān, date 1155 A.H. = 1745. H 0·45
67. Lamp, blue, green, and yellow ornaments on white ground. H 0·29
68. Lamp, blue and green decoration on white enamel. (Mosque of Seyyid El-Bedawy, at Tanta.) H 0·23
69. Lamp, blue decoration on white ground. (Same provenance.) H 0·22
70. Lamp of terra cotta covered with turquoise blue enamel. (Mosque of Sultan Hasan.) H 0·30
71. Large vessel of terra cotta, glazed, and decorated with a network of lines. Evidently made in several distinct zones. (Mosque El-Azhar.) H 0·91
72. Cup glazed inside. D 0·06
73—80. Fragments of glazed pottery: 73, 74, inscriptions; L 0·07. 75, armorial bearing, a sword on an escutcheon, and inscription; L 0·08. 76, inscription; L 0·07. 77, fleur-de-lys; D 0·07. 78, white glaze upon terra cotta, on bottom غيبي Gheyby; D 0·09. 79, similar, on bottom غزال Ghazzāl; D 0·03. 80, foliate ornament of Arab character; L 0·09. (Given by M. Herz Bey, 1893.)
81—166. Objects and fragments of pottery: 81—108, fragments, opaque white glaze; 135, design resembling porcelain fragment no. 318; 144, green glaze of celadon class; fragment with cockscomb still attached which supported another object in the kiln; 157, cup, white glaze, D 0·13; 158, 159, cups, D 0·16, 0·11; 160—162, small vessels, H 0·07—0·10; 163, 164, camps, H 0·09; 165, blue glaze, D 0·03; 166, saucer. D 0·04 (Given by Dr. Fouquet, 1893.)

POTTERY 71

ROOM VI.
—167. Plaque representing the Haram and Kaaba at
Mecca, in perspective, with inscription stating
it was made by Mohammad Esh-Sha'my (the
Syrian) in 1139 A.H.=1726.   L 0·45

VI. 167. THE KAABA IN TILEWORK

168—177. Ten enamelled tiles with ornament derived from the violet.   L 0·25

72 CATALOGUE OF THE ARAB MUSEUM

Room VI.
178. Piece of enamelled border. H 0·13
179—181. Four pieces of a spandrel. L 0·25
182—185. Five enamelled tiles, white ornament on blue ground. L 0·24
186, 187. Two fragments of wall-tiles, enamelled in red, blue, and green, on white ground. H 0·14, 0·17
188—190. Three tiles enamelled with two shades of blue on white ground. L 0·25

VI. 172. Enamelled Tile

191. Plaque containing a portion of a panel and frame. L 0·25
192—195. Four oblong tiles, with blue, grey, and green ornament on white ground. L 0·19
196. Tile with grey and blue ornament in several shades. L 0·19
197—199. Three tiles with white and green ornament on blue ground. L 0·13—0·15
200—212. Thirteen tiles. L 0·10—0·23 poor work.
213, 214. Two pieces: a panel in white bordered by blue and green ornament. L 0·25 poor work.
215—228. Fourteen tiles of good workmanship. L 0·11—0·25

Room VI.

229, 230. Two tiles (one imperfect) with interlacing border in relief.[1] (Mosque of Khōshkadam El-Ahmady.) L 0·06, 0·10

231—235. Five panels formed of fifty tiles, representing a flower growing out of a vase. (House of Nefūsa Gasūsa, modern.) L 0·79

236—247. Twelve tiles. Modern. L 0·20

248—252. Tiles with naturalistic designs:—an insect, cyprus, foliage, and flowers. European.

253—271. Nineteen tiles with white letters on blue ground forming the *kalima* or profession of faith and pious formulas.

272. Large arched panel composed (now) of fourteen small tiles, on which are inscriptions in white letters outlined in green on blue ground, framed in border of white on green.

273. Part of a panel containing medallion in honour of a sultān, white on blue.

274. Piece identical with lower part of preceding no.

275—292. Eighteen enamelled tiles with blue letters and ornaments outlined with white on blue ground; the letters extend over two courses of tiles.

293—308. Forty enamelled tiles with white inscription extending over two courses, and white ornaments of pure Arab style, on blue ground. (Dome, demolished 1860, of Tomb-mosque of El-Ghūry, 1503.)

309. Fragment of brown tile with white inscription and green foilage. (Dome of Khawand Baraka, xiv. c.)

310—313. Part of cornice of frieze. (Same provenance.)

---

[1] Similar tiles are in the mosque of Sheykhū. They resemble those of Spain, whence they were probably imported.

74 CATALOGUE OF THE ARAB MUSEUM

Room VI.
314—317. Tiles, four green, five white, two brown (dark and light), from north minaret of mosque of Sultān En-Nāsir Mohammad in the Citadel, 1318.

C. Porcelain

318. Part of a porcelain vessel, white, with bright blue foilage. (Rubbish heaps.)
319—322. Four celadon vases. (Mosque of Sultān Hasan.)
323. Twenty-three blue enamel beads.

Miscellaneous

324. Stone lamp. Given by Dr. Schweinfurth.
325. Plaster cup.
326. Carnelian dish, with edges raised, cut in facets. (Mosque of Kalāūn.) A precious example of the work in crystal and precious stones chiefly known only from medieval historians and travellers.
327. Modern lantern.

ROOM VII.

A. Meshrebīya Work

Room VII.
1. Front of meshrebīya window or balcony: in upper panel a vase between two lions. H 1·59
2. Side of balcony. H 3·00
3—5. Parts of balcony, the base in fretted wood. H 2·34, 3·20
6. Front of balcony. H 2·65
7. Side of balcony with small window. H 2·30
8. Ten carved balusters from staircase. L 0·65
9. Side of chair. L 0·69
10. Staircase, bases and capitals of balusters carved with arabesques. L 2·30
11. In the upper panel, two animals. H 1·54
12. Side of balcony with small window. H 2·74
13. Front of balcony with projecting window (khōkha). L 3·00
14—17. Turned work. L 0·53—0·55
18. Side of balcony. H 2·85
19. Side of balcony with window. H 3·50
20. Turned lattice with large knobs. H 1·95
21. Side of balcony with base. H 2·00
22. Turned lattice. H 1·85
23. Side of balcony with khōkha. H 1·93
24. Korān-reader's seat. H 1·63
25. Lattice, with representation of pulpit and lamp. H 1·53

Room VII.
26. Two sides of balcony.   H 1·05
27. Window lattice with large knobs.   H 1·12
28. Turned lattice.   L 0·73

VII. 1.   Panel of Meshrebīya

29. Turned lattice, with triangular knobs ornamented with ebony buttons.   H 0·43
30. Korān lectern. (Mosque of El-Muayyad, 1420.) H 1·20

Room VII.

B. Lath Trellis

31. Lattice in cut wood.
32. Trellis, octagonal mesh. L 0·75
33. Trellis, cruciform mesh. H 0·93
34. Trellis, octagonal and cruciform meshes. H 1·00
35. Trellis, star-shaped mesh. H 1·35
36. Trellis, star-shaped and cruciform meshes. H 0·60

C. Doors

37. Leaves of a wall-cupboard (*dulāb*) ornamented with arcades above. H 1·70
38. Door of panel-work. H 1·64
39. Front of a five-doored cupboard (*dulāb*); three designs of pannelling. L 3·35
40. Front of a cupboard surmounted by arches. H 1·65
41. Door, wavy pattern. H 1·07
42. Door panelled in rhomboids and diamonds. H 0·95
43. Door panelled in rectangles. H 1·00
44. Door panelled in sixfoil design. H 1·80
45, 46. Front of cupboard, tenfoil design. H 1·76
47. Three cupboard fronts; the middle with hexagonal design. H 1·75
48, 49. Cupboard doors panelled in steps. H 1·08
50. Cupboard door, rectangular design. H 1·08
51, 52. Cupboard door, hexagonal design. H 1·08
53, 54. Cupboard door, rectangular design. H 1·08
55. Korān lectern, cut out of a single piece. (Mosque of El-Muayyad, 1420.) H 1·00

D. Lanterns

56. Cylindrical lantern in six tiers, composed of open-work panels containing arabesques and geometrical designs; except the third tier

ROOM VII.

where the panels are solid and carved with an inscription in honour of Sultān El-Ghūry, and are divided by medallions also containing his name and titles; dome-top, surmounted by crescent. Early xvi c. H 1·55

57. Twelve-sided lantern in six tiers; open-work panels with geometrical designs; dome surmounted by crescent, with inscription in name of قيسون الملكى الناصرى 'Keysūn [the mamlūk] of El-Melik en-Nāsir'; and on the third tier the inscription عمل المعلم بدر ابو يعلا فى شهور سنة ثلاثين وسبعمائة 'Made by the master Bedr Abū-Ya'lā in the months of the year 730 (1329),' and فرغ مدة اربعطشر (*sic*) يوم 'Finished in the space of fourteen days.' (Mosque of Sultān Hasan, 1358.)

58. Lantern; the lower part in form of a plate with twelve sockets is attached by three chains to the dome, which is of open-work and surmounted by a crescent, and has projecting arms for lamps. H 2·00

ROOM VIII.

BOOKBINDINGS

ARAB bookbinding is interesting not only in itself, but on account of its influence on Italian and European binders from the XVth c.[1] The three hundred bindings in the Museum, with the exception of a few specimens from the mosque of Barkūk, were all found piled together among books in a small room behind the *mihrāb* of the mosque of El-Muayyad, and probably belonged to the library originally established in that mosque. Oriental bindings have a flat instead of a rounded edge, which is generally protected by a flap on which as much ornament is lavished as on the side; the side does not project beyond the edge of the book. The material is generally marocco, but silk and other tissues are sometimes used in the decoration. The leather is generally left its natural colour and only painted

---

[1] The early Italian bindings belonging to Maioli, Canevarius, Grollier, and especially Corvinus, are obviously indebted to Arab models. The bindings at Budapesth which formed part of the library of Mathias Corvinus (1458—1490), and were carried off to Constantinople in the xvi c., and only restored to Hungary in 1878, are so Oriental in character that one would almost believe they were made in the East.

in certain places. The *Arab* bindings are marked by arabesque ornament applied by the iron and forming intaglio designs on the sides, even though the ornament on the guards be in relief. The side ornament is sometimes contrasted by colour and gold from the guards which retain the original colour. Often a foliate design is cut out in leather and applied on a silk ground and touched up with gold previously laid on the outlines, and pressed with hot iron, with very happy effect (see below). The designs are very similar to those of other branches of Arab art; on the sides polygonal patterns and inscriptions are most usual, but arabesques on the guards. The Museum is rich in arabesques and geometrical patterns, but for inscriptions the visitor must go to the Khedivial Library and study the magnificent bindings of Korāns, dating from the XIIIth c. This fine manner of work ended with the Turkish conquest of Egypt. *Turkish* bindings have this vital distinction from the Arab style, that, instead of heated irons, mechanical dies or *matrices* were employed, and the individual taste of the artist was thereby deprived of free play in tooling. Arabesques and geometrical designs gave place to naturalistic figures of the Persian style, and effects were obtained in the way of high relief by means of two thicknesses of leather, one above the other, the upper being cut out to the desired shape. The leather was then forcibly pressed against the mould, and obtained the sharp relief which marks the Persian and Turkish style of binding. These moulds were originally of camel-leather, but at a later period they were made of metal, as is shown by three brass moulds in the collection of J. A. Cattaui Bey of Cairo. *Varnished* bindings form the most modern variety. The leather was coated with a sort of plaster, on which the design, most commonly flowers in their natural colours, were painted, and the surface was then varnished. The varnish turned yellow in time, but where it scales the painting appears in its original freshness.

Room VIII.
Case A. (67 Specimens)

1. Flap of a leather binding, covered with green tissue, with pinked ornament tooled with foliage picked out in gold.
2. Side of leather binding; in centre, geometrical rosette in various colours and gold.
3. Flap of a large binding, with impressed ornament. L. 082
4, 5. Guards of leather binding, ornamented with arabesques in the natural colour upon a darker pressed ground.
6. Side of a leather binding ornamented with geometrical designs; in the centre a twelve-foiled rosette, and quarter rosettes at angles; the alternate foils marked by gold points.
7. Flap of leather binding, ornamented with interlaced gold and leather pattern, enclosed in wide geometrical border.
8. Side of a leather binding, Turkish (in Persian style); oval centre-piece, whence leaves and flowers spread out in relief; edges set off by gold lines.

ROOM VIII.

CASE B. (204 Specimens)

9. Flap of binding like no. 1.
10. Side of binding entirely covered with geometrical designs.
11. Wooden Korān-case, covered with leather, with a repoussé gilt leather rosette on the top, and a richly gilt band at the base, bearing an inscription in which the name Kansūh (probably Kansūh El-Ghūry, 1501—1516) may still be read. The interior is divided into three compartments, each with ten grooves, for the *ajzā*.

12. Embroidered silk stuff.
13. Tomb-cover of red cloth with appliqué velvet and silk.
14. Lantern, dome of brass filigree work, supporting a plate of nine sockets; and chased with numerous inscriptions, in which are the name and titles of 'the deceased' (المرحوم) Sultān En-Nāsir Mohammad.

PASSAGE, 1. DOOR FROM EL-AZHAR, CIRC. 1000

[*To face* p. 83](

PASSAGE

Woodwork

PASSAGE

1. Folding door with panels carved with ornamen and kufic inscriptions,[1]

    on the right leaf,   on the left leaf,

    الامام الحاكم بامر الله   مولانا امير المؤمنين
    ابائه الطاهرين وابنائه   صلوات الاه عليه وعلى

    'Our lord the Commander of the Faithful—
      the Imām El-Hākim bi-amri-llāh,
    Blessings of God upon him and upon—
      his pure ancestors and descendants.'

    (Mosque El-Azhar. The Fātimid Caliph El-Hākim reigned 996—1020.)   H 3·20

2. Front of a balcony of carved wood.   L 2·56
3. Side of balcony with small projecting window. H 1·95
4. Folding door carved with representations of men and animals. (Cp. Room IV, no. 54.) (Mosque of Kalāūn, 1284.)   H 3·83
5. Door carved with inscriptions at top and bottom

---

[1] There are marks of clumsy restoration on these fine old doors; the panels have been misplaced, and the inscriptions on the left leaf ought to be on the right, and vice versâ; the framework has been entirely renewed, and also some of the panels.

PASSAGE

and ornament in the middle. (Mosque El-Ghārīya in El-Azhar, 1440. See 44 of Room V.) L 1·30
6. Large folding door richly carved with geometrical designs. (Damietta.) H 4·15
7. Folding door with filigree chased bronze plating. (Mosque of El-Higāzīya, 1360.)
8. Side of meshrebīya balcony; lower part fretwork. H 2·30
9. Front of meshrebīya balcony with five glass and stucco windows above. H 2·60
10. Leaf of a door studded with nails. (Tomb-mosque of El-Ghūry, 1503.) H 2·95
11. Piece of board carved with ornaments and inscriptions. L 2·62
12. Piece of carved board from a ceiling. L 0·80
13. Brass-wire trellis. H 0·97
14. Front of a balcony with three windows; base of turned work with cube knobs, of the style called '*mamūny.*' H 1·75
15. Carved joist. (Tomb-mosque of El-Ghūry, 1503.) L 2·88
16. Carved board with traces of gilding. L 2·80
17—22. Carved boards. (Tomb-mosque of El-Ghūry.) L 1·05—2·80
23. Wooden ceiling with geometrical pattern of fillets (beads) nailed on. L 3·20
24—26. Carved ceiling boards. (Mosque of El-Māridāny, 1338.) L 1·60—2·53
27—34. Ceiling boards carved in relief. (Medresa of Barkūk, 1384.)
35. Carved ceiling board. (Tomb-mosque of El-Ghūry.) L 2·80
36. Part of round window casing, carved. (Mosque of El-Māridāny.) W 0·20
37. Two fragments of large carved inscription. L 1·78

PASSAGE

38. Twenty-five carved ceiling boards. (Mosque of El-Māridāny.) L 1·50—2·47
39. Eight pieces of stalactite from a ceiling. H 0·65
40. Two pieces of a frieze with ornament and inscription in stucco, painted and gilt. L 2·73
41. Panelled door. H 1·90
42. Folding door, panelled and inlaid with ivory. H 2·48, repaired.
43—47. Carved boards. (Tomb-mosque of El-Ghūry.)
48. Front of meshrebīya balcony with three windows. L 2·37
49. Piece of board carved with ornament and inscriptions. L 2·27
50. Door-leaf studded with nails in geometrical patterns. (Tomb-mosque of El-Ghūry.) H 2·95
51. Front of balcony with five windows. L 3·52
52. Side of balcony with oblong window; base, fretwork. H 2·82
53. Base of balcony with rosettes, turned and fretted. L 2·54
54. Railing of geometrical design. L 2·12
55. Folding door with panels of different woods carved with kufic and naskhy inscriptions. (Tomb of Es-Sālih Ayyūb, 1249.) H 4·35
56. Panelled doors. H 2·15
57. Front of balcony. L 2·50
58. Lintel of shop door, in turned and carved panels, with name of Kāït-Bey, late xv c. (Wekāla of Kāït-Bey, in the Gemālīya.) L 2·68
59. Side of a meshrebīya balcony, with small bay. H 1·50
60. Front of a meshrebīya balcony, with base and panel. L 2·35
61. Carved ceiling joist. (Tomb-mosque of El-Ghūry, 1503.) L 4·80

PASSAGE

62. Folding door with geometrical bronze plating or inscriptions. (Mosque of El-Higāzīya, 1360.) H 4·20
63. Beam carved with inscription in name of Sheykh Mohammad 'Abd-el-Latīf, A.H. 1178=1764. L 3·82
64—68. Panels of turned wood. L 0·62—1·22
69. Ten ceiling boards. L 0·80—1·90
70. Four doors with carved ornament. (Wekāla Sunbul, Beyn-es-Sūreyn, demolished 1884.) H 1·40—1·53
71. Lintel of shop door with turned and carved panels and name of Kāït-Bey. (Wekāla of Kāït-Bey, late xv c.) L 2·57
72. Inscribed panel. L 1·0
73. Two pieces of large inscriptional board. L 0·70—1·05
74. Five pieces of frieze with kufic inscription from inner partitions of mosque of Ibn-Tūlūn. 886. L 1·06—1·40
75. Part of a ceiling from the arch of a porch. (Mosque of Ibn-Tūlūn.) L 0·82
76. Part of pulpit staircase (of Lāgīn, 1296, in mosque of Ibn-Tūlūn.) L 0·98
77. Wood ornamented with fretwork. Modern. (Mosque of Seyyida Zeyneb, 1760.) L 2·11
78. Two wooden corbels of a house. Modern. L 1·63
79. Lantern in form of hexagonal prism. Modern. H 1·00
80. Brass vessel. H 0·30
81. Brass lantern. Modern. D 0·25
82. Brass vessel. H 0·30
83. Brass lantern for five lamps, filigree dome. H 0·55
84. Brass vessel. H 0·70
85. Brass lantern for seven lamps, with dome, chased. H 0·70

WOODWORK, ETC.

PASSAGE
86. Brass lantern, conical, with bulb, chased with inscriptions and ornament.   H 0·75
87. Brass lantern with tray.   H 2·20
88. Chair of turned and carved panelwork.   H 1·50
89. Four dove-tails. (Mosque of Aksunkur, 1347.) L 0·19—0·37

PASSAGE, 86.   BRASS LANTERN

90. Settle (*dikka*) of turned and worked wood. L 2·43
91. Board with large inscription in relief. (Mosque El-Azhar.)

PASSAGE

92. Board with inscription امر بتجديد هذا الجامع سيدنا ومولانا السلطان الملك الاشرف ابو النصر قائتباى خلد الله ملكه ' Ordered the restoration of this mosque our lord and master the Sultān El-Melik el-Ashraf Abu-n-Nasr Kāït-Bey, God prolong his reign!' Late xv c.
93. Board carved with inscription from Korān, and also relating to erection of a *miḥrāb* in 753 A.H. = 1352.
94. Board with inscription referring to gift of a Korān by Bedr Lulu, in 858 A.H. = 1454.
95. Panel with inscription referring to the building of a mosque.

ANNEX I.

1—7. Panelled doors. H 1·75—2·25
8. Secret door forming cupboard. H 1·90
9. Folding door, plated with copper and ornamented with bronze stars. (Mosque of Talāi' ibn Ruzzīk, 1160.) H 4·37
10. Folding door with bronze plating. (Tomb of Imām Esh-Shāfi'y, 1211.) H 3·23
11. Folding door with remains of bronze plating in centre. H 4·50
12. Leaf of a window-shutter plated with copper, framed with bronze at top and bottom, and cut fleurs-de-lis. H 3·55
13, 14. Folding shutters of panel-work, chased bronze hinges, and inscriptions at top. (Mosque of Suleymān Pasha at Citadel. xvi c.) H 2·25
15. Folding doors with copper hinges and cast-bronze flowers. H 3·25
16. Folding doors with remains of filigree bronze border. H 3·07
17. Four doors with remains of bronze plating and two knockers. H 3·17
18. Leaf of door of wood, with inscriptions and rosette in cast-bronze filigree work. (Mosque of El-Muayyad, 1420.) H 3·44
19—23. Folding doors plated with filigree cast-bronze. Modern. (Mosque of Seyyida Zeyneb, 1760.) H 2·28—3·20
24, 25. Chairs of turned wood. L 1·70, 1·36

90 CATALOGUE OF THE ARAB MUSEUM

ANNEX I.

26, 27. Korān-readers' chairs of panelling and ivory inlay. L 1·55, 1·25
28 –31. Lecterns for Korān. (Mosque of El-Muayyad, 1420.) H 1·11, 1·12, 1·00, 1·00
32. Lectern of turned wood. H 1·20
33. Pulpit (*minbar*) of rich geometrical panelling inlaid with ivory, and turned balustrade to staircase. (Mosque of El-Higāzīya, 1360.)
34, 35. Inlaid wooden boxes. L 0·76
36. Wooden casing of a tomb (top wanting) with carved inscription. (Tomb in the street Dely Hoseyn.) L 1·90
37. Three sides of a similar tomb-casing. L 1·26
38. Five panels, the centre bearing name of Kāït-Bey. Late xv c. (Tomb of Esh-Shāfi'y.) L 2·10
39. Front of meshrebīya balcony. L 1·68
40. Side of balcony, cubic knobs ('mamūny' work). H 1·86
41. Front of a six-panelled piece of furniture, with pilasters in middle.
42. Partition of turned and carved wood, with geometrical patterns. (Mosque of Ibn-el-Bakry, in the Hārat el-Utūf.) L 4·08
43. Soffit of a door, in three planes, finely carved. L 2·40
44. Stalactites in triple grades of gilt wood. H 0·40
45. Staircase and balustrades of a pulpit carved with arabesques on string-board and raisers and on cubic knobs of balustrade. (Mosque of Kūsūn, 1329.)
46. Panel of carved wood open-work. Side 0·48
47. Three plates of chased copper from a door.
48—50. Stucco and coloured glass window-lights. L 0·84, 1·30, 0·65
51—53. Base of a marble column, *kulla* form : 53 has foliage or corners of plinth. H 0·12, 0·28, 0·42

Annex I.

54. Byzantine foliate capital. H 0·45
55. Capital of an angle pillar of a marble tomb. H 0·50
56. Forty-two fragments of sculptured marble. H 0·30—1·20
57. Marble slab, in two fragments, sculptured with titles of a sultān, and two chimaeras addorsed. (Tomb in Mosque of El-Muayyad, 1420.) W 0·73
58. Marble sculptured with four fish. L 2·20
59. Twelve pieces of sculptured stone. L 0·28—0·53 (56—59 were all found in the Mosque of El-Muayyad during the recent restoration.)
60. Leaf of a panelled door, cast-bronze filigree work at top and bottom, bronze rosette in centre.
61. Parapet of ten panels of turned woodwork.

The Second Room of this Annex and the whole of Annex II are occupied by *over a thousand tombstones*, with kufic inscriptions, chiefly of the II—IVth c. of the Hijra, from the old cemetery at Aswān and that south of Cairo: most of them were the gift of the Direction of the Gîza Museum.

Sampson Low, Marston & Company's

PUBLICATIONS.

NOW COMPLETE.
THE QUEEN'S PRIME MINISTERS.
A Series of Political Biographies. Edited by Stuart J. Reid.

** *A limited Library Edition of* **Two Hundred and Fifty Copies,** *each numbered, printed on hand-made paper, parchment binding, gilt-top, with facsimile reproductions, in some cases of characteristic notes of Speeches and Letters, which are not included in the ordinary Edition, and some additional portraits.*

Price for the Complete Set of NINE VOLUMES, Four Guineas nett.
No Volumes of this Edition Sold separately.

THE EARL OF BEACONSFIELD, K.G. By JAMES ANTHONY FROUDE, D.C.L. With Photogravure Portrait. Fifth Edition. Crown 8vo, cloth, 3s. 6d.

LORD MELBOURNE. By HENRY DUNCKLEY ("VERAX"). With Photogravure Portrait. Crown 8vo, 3s. 6d.

THE RIGHT HON. W. E. GLADSTONE, M.P. By G. W. E. RUSSELL. New Edition. Twelfth Thousand. With Photogravure Portrait. Crown 8vo, 3s. 6d.

THE MARQUIS OF SALISBURY, K.G. By H. D. TRAILL, D.C.L. With Photogravure Portrait. Second Edition. Cr. 8vo, 3s. 6d.

SIR ROBERT PEEL. By JUSTIN MCCARTHY, M.P. With Photogravure Portrait. Crown 8vo, 3s. 6d.

LORD PALMERSTON. By the MARQUIS OF LORNE. Second Edition. With Photogravure Portrait. Crown 8vo, 3s. 6d.

THE EARL OF DERBY. By GEORGE SAINTSBURY. With Photogravure Portrait. Crown 8vo, 3s. 6d.

THE EARL OF ABERDEEN. By BARON STANMORE. With Portrait. Crown 8vo, 3s. 6d.

LORD JOHN RUSSELL. By STUART J. REID. Second Edition. With Portrait. Crown 8vo, 3s. 6d.

SAINTS AND THEIR SYMBOLS.

A Companion in the Churches and Picture Galleries of Europe. By E. A. GREENE. Ninth Edition, Revised. With several Illustrations. Cloth extra, gilt, red edges, 3s. 6d.

LONDON: SAMPSON LOW, MARSTON & COMPANY, LTD.,
ST. DUNSTAN'S HOUSE, FETTER LANE, FLEET STREET E.C.

By STANLEY LANE-POOLE.

THE LIFE OF THE RT. HON. STRATFORD CANNING, VISCOUNT STRATFORD DE REDCLIFFE, K.G. From his Memoirs and Papers. Three Portraits. Library Edition. 2 vols. 8vo, pp. xxix. 519; xviii. 475.
Popular Edition. pp. xx. 377.

THE LIFE OF SIR HARRY PARKES, K.C.B., G.C.M.G., H. B. M. Minister to China and Japan. Portrait and Maps. 2 vols. pp. xxviii. 512; xxi. 477.

SIR RICHARD CHURCH, C.B., G.C.H., Commander-in-Chief of the Greeks in the War of Independence. With two Plans. 8vo, pp. iv. 73.

THE LIFE OF EDWARD WILLIAM LANE. 8vo, pp. 138.

THE SPEECHES AND TABLE-TALK OF THE PROPHET MOHAMMAD. 18mo, pp. lxiii. 196. Golden Treasury Series.

AURANGZIB. Rulers of India Series. 8vo, pp. 212.

THE MOHAMMADAN DYNASTIES: Chronological and Genealogical Tables. 8vo, pp. xxviii. 361.

THE MOORS IN SPAIN. Illustrated. 8vo, pp. xx. 285.

TURKEY. Illustrated. 8vo, pp. xix. 373.

THE BARBARY CORSAIRS. Illustrated. 8vo, pp. xviii. 316.

THE HISTORY OF THE MOGHUL EMPERORS ILLUSTRAT BY THEIR COINS. pp. clxxvii.

STUDIES IN A MOSQUE. Second Edition. 8vo, pp. viii. 326.

THE ART OF THE SARACENS IN EGYPT. Illustrated. 8vo. pp. xviii. 264. Published for the Committee of Council on Education.

CAIRO: SKETCHES OF ITS HISTORY, MONUMENTS, AND SOCIAL LIFE. Illustrated. 8vo, pp. xiv. 320.

CATALOGUE OF ORIENTAL AND INDIAN COINS IN THE BRITISH MUSEUM. Printed by order of the Trustees. (Ouvrage couronné par l'Institut de France.) 8vo, 13 vols. pp. dlxv., 3872.

LANE'S ARABIC-ENGLISH LEXICON. Edited by Stanley Lane-Poole. Imp. 4to, 8 vols. pp. xcii. 3064.

GILBERT & RIVINGTON
Limited

Oriental, Classical and General Printers

TRANSLATORS,

TYPEFOUNDERS, BOOKBINDERS, &c.

PRINTERS TO THE EGYPT EXPLORATION FUND,
THE BRITISH MUSEUM, INDIA OFFICE,
&c., &c.

Printing by Moveable Types in any Language,
ANCIENT OR MODERN.

PRINTERS OF LANE'S ARABIC LEXICON.

— SPECIMEN OF TYPE —
(HIEROGLYPHICS)

(Cleopatra's Needle (c. 1450 B.C.)

Specimens of Type

COPTIC

ⲛⲓⲁ ⲛⲉⲛⲓⲟⲟⲩ ⲁⲛ ⲉⲛⲁⲍⲉ ⲛⲉ ⲛⲥⲟⲫⲟⲥ ⲟⲩⲁⲉ
ⲛⲥⲁⲗⲟ ⲁⲛ ⲛⲉⲧⲥⲟⲟⲩⲛ ⲛϩⲣⲁⲓ. ⲉⲧⲃⲉ ⲡⲁⲓ ⲁⲓϫⲟⲟⲥ
ϫⲉ ⲥⲓⲟⲧⲛ ⲉⲣⲟⲓ ⲧⲁϫⲱ ⲙⲡⲉⲧⲓ ⲙⲡⲉⲧⲥⲟⲟⲩⲛ ⲙⲙⲟⲟⲩ
ⲛⲓ ⲅⲁⲣ ⲉⲛⲁϣⲁϫⲉ.

Ⲟⲩⲉⲅⲕⲱⲙⲓⲟⲛ ⲉ̀ ⲁϥⲧⲁⲟⲩⲟϥ ⲛ̀ϫⲉ ⲡⲓⲁ̀ⲅⲓⲟⲥ
ⲓⲱⲁⲛⲛⲏⲥ ⲡⲓⲭⲣⲏⲥⲟⲥⲧⲟⲙⲟⲥ... ⲉ̀ⲡⲓⲥⲕⲟⲡⲟⲥ
ⲛ̀ⲧⲉ ⲡⲕⲱⲥⲧⲁⲛⲧⲓⲛⲟⲩⲡⲟⲗⲓⲥ ⲉ̀ ⲡⲓⲛⲓϣϯ ⲙ̀
ⲡⲣⲟⲫⲏⲧⲏⲥ ⲡⲓⲁ̀ⲅⲟⲥ ⲏ̀ⲗⲓⲁⲥ ⲡⲓⲑⲉⲥⲃⲩⲧⲏⲥ

ARABIC

اَلْحَمْدُ لِلّٰهِ رَبِّ ٱلْعَالَمِيْنَ ٱلرَّحْمٰنِ ٱلرَّحِيْمِ

راح زيد طاعناً فى سنه   وانبرى عمرو يذاجيه فتى
قال شيخ الحارة الهم الذى   شهد الشيب عليه بلفف

TURKISH

تهى دست قپویه وارسن افندى اوور دبرلر الکده پیشکش اولسه
افندم بیور دیرار
ایولاك ایله دکزه براق دکزبیلمز ایسه خالق بیاور   دل قلیجدن چوق اولدرر

CUNEIFORM

𒐕 𒀸 𒐕 𒀸𒈪 𒂊𒀭𒁺 𒐕𒌋𒌋𒌋 𒀸𒈪𒐕𒐕 𒀸𒂊𒐕 𒈫𒈫 𒊺

𒀸𒁁 𒐏 𒈪𒐕𒐕 𒀸𒁁 𒌋 𒀸 𒂊𒐕𒐕

GILBERT AND RIVINGTON
Limited
ST. JOHN'S HOUSE, CLERKENWELL, LONDON, E.C.